LESSONS FROM BRADLEY

Discovering God's Blessing In All Things

For Karen —
God bless you!

Heather Wanemaker ☺

Rom. 8:28

LESSONS FROM BRADLEY

Discovering God's Blessing In All Things

Heather Wanamaker

Parson Place Press
Mobile, Alabama

Lessons from Bradley: Discovering God's Blessing in All Things by Heather Wanamaker

Copyright © 2013 by Heather Wanamaker.
All rights reserved.

Cover Design by Just Ink Digital Design

ISBN 13: 978-0-9888528-1-5

Library of Congress Control Number: 2013931521

Dedication

This book is affectionately dedicated to my husband, Scott, my love, my friend, and my teammate in this adventure called life. I love you deeply and am so grateful God chose you for me. Thank you for loving me, loving our family, and, most importantly, for loving the Lord.

Contents

Acknowledgements

An endeavor of this sort would not be possible without the support and assistance of many people. First of all, I would like to thank my family and dear friends for their love and support. I treasure the blessing you are to me. Each of you holds a special place in my heart.

I am indebted to my mentor and friend, Reverend James Lee Beall. Thank you for your guidance on this project and years of faithfully teaching the Word of God. My growth in Christ is, in large measure, a result of your sound teaching. What a privilege and honor it has been for me to work with you!

I would also like to extend special thanks to Susan Bulat. Thank you for sharing your literary expertise by proofreading my manuscript and encouraging me along every step of this journey. I am appreciative of your love and support.

To my dear sisters in Christ, my prayer group, thank you for holding my family and me up in prayer throughout the years. Also, thank you for bathing this labor of love in prayer from its inception until now. It has been a pleasure to grow in His grace alongside you.

I am grateful for Bradley's teachers, therapists, and para-professionals, past and present. Thank you for your selfless love and care shown to Bradley, and us, throughout the years. We are blessed to have such excellent educational opportunities available for Bradley. The personnel of Glen H. Peters School and Keith Bovenschen School are second to none. Each of these individuals has made a unique, valued contribution to our life with Bradley at some point.

Foreword

The topic of suffering has puzzled humanity for ages. People, including Christians, have questioned the equity of God and even His loving nature. How can a loving God allow calamity to befall mankind, let alone His chosen people? My husband and I became acquainted with the subject of suffering in a way we would never have chosen (as if any of us would choose to suffer), with the birth of our oldest son, Bradley, who is nearing fifteen years old.

Suffering rocks our world and upsets us in ways nothing else can. We are most vulnerable (and often confused) in our time of need. There are influential teachers in the Christian world today who misrepresent the truth of Scripture. They claim the life of a Christian should be free of problems. They claim our lives should be full of the blessings we would choose for ourselves. But is that really the case?

They place a burden on those who are suffering that our Heavenly Father never intended. They imply the reason God doesn't heal you or your loved one is due to your lack of faith. You are left to wonder, *If I just had more faith, would God heal me or my loved one?* Is it possible that God has bigger plans and purposes at work?

You may be in the midst of one of life's trials right now. You may be watching a friend or loved one face enormous challenges – or you may be in a season of life where the days are sunny and carefree. Whatever your situation, it is my prayer that you will be encouraged by reading this story. Encouraged to keep going if you are the one providing what seems like never-ending care. Encouraged to come alongside that blindsided friend or loved one to give support. Encouraged to seek an eternal perspective and not become disillusioned when troubles come. Yes, *when* they come, not *if* they come.

My purpose in writing this book is not to give a theological treatise on suffering (I will leave that to the theologians), nor am I seeking a pity party for the situation we find ourselves in with my son. My purpose is simply to share our story. Specifically, I want you, dear reader, to see how God has brought good from a heartbreaking situation and perhaps to encourage those facing similar situations.

I believe God uses the experience of suffering in believers to produce the fruit of maturity and the development of Christian character. In this book, you will enter God's unique classroom chosen specifically for my family. Your classroom will look different, but the Teacher will be the same.

Heather Wanamaker
Autumn 2012

Introduction

In the early fall of 1997, I discovered I was pregnant. My husband, Scott, and I were thrilled with the news. We joyfully looked forward to the arrival of our first child. At the same time, however, I was also apprehensive. I felt hugely inadequate as a Christian mother.

I did not grow up in a Christian home. My parents separated and divorced by the time I was two years old, forcing my mother to work full time to support my older sister and me. My father abandoned us completely. Perhaps due to a combined motivation of guilt over our circumstances and the popular parenting advice of the day, my mother's parenting style was permissive. Generally speaking, I did what I wanted when I wanted. When I was told there was something I could not do, I figured out how to do what I wanted anyway. I became accustomed to having things my way and unconsciously carried this unrealistic expectation into young adulthood.

My only exposure to church as a child was limited to when I went to visit my grandmothers and a few other times. Scott's family was very different. His family faithfully attended church services and he accepted Christ as Savior at an early age. When we were dating, we started attending church together and later, I became a Christian during my senior year of high school. We married the following year and continued to attend church regularly. Still, I really knew very little about the Bible. I was afraid that our child, within a short time of attendance in Sunday school, would know more than I did. How was I going to answer his or her inevitable questions when I didn't even know the answers myself? The thought of the embarrassment of my child knowing more about the Bible than I did drove me to ask the Lord in prayer to teach me more about Him. Although avoiding embarrassment was my initial motive for seeking the Lord, He used that desire to draw me closer to Him. Yes, I had accepted Him as my Lord and Savior, but now I really wanted to KNOW Him in a way I never had before. A hunger for His Word began to grow in me. He began to prepare me for what lay ahead. It is against this backdrop of my life that our story begins.

A short time prior to my due date, Scott and I went out for dinner. We like Chinese food, so we selected a restaurant close to our home. At the end of our dinner, we cracked open our fortune cookies. We didn't believe that fortune cookies held any magical power to predict the future. We didn't give any weight to what they had to say. We just read them for entertainment. I unfolded the little piece of paper in my cookie and read my "fortune." It read, "A challenge is near." We chuckled and I thought, *Well, **yeah**! Nobody ever said that labor is easy.*

I saved my "fortune" to show our son or daughter in the future what was said about him or her. I had no idea how true that little piece of paper would turn out to be.

Chapter 1 – The Storm

My husband and I stood looking down at our newborn son. We were standing in an isolation room at the edge of his isolette trying to mentally digest all that was happening. There were tubes and wires everywhere – multiple IV's, catheters, monitors, probes. A ventilator tube was coming from his mouth. A tube was going up his nose down into his stomach for feedings. His striking, beautiful blonde hair was wrapped in gauze. The scene was surreal. I was functioning, but felt as if I was walking in a dream. It would be many months before I realized the extent of what all this meant.

The storm began as many storms do. Calm, blue skies signaled pleasant, joyful times. Then a front moved into the region, bringing with it increasing wind speeds. The winds were followed by rain, which was, at times, a torrential downpour of emotions.

On May 19, 1998, at 3:00 in the afternoon, I went for a routine obstetrical visit. My husband, Scott, and I were delighted to be expecting our first child within a matter of days. After experiencing a miscarriage the previous year, we looked forward to the day of our child's arrival. We were eager to receive one of God's greatest blessings. I had listened intently to Christian radio programs devoted to the subject of child rearing. I wanted my child to experience the blessing of growing up in a Christian home. I sincerely wanted to be a good, Christ-like example for my new son or daughter. I prayed for God to draw me closer to Him, to teach me His Word.

Scott's mother accompanied me to the appointment. She was staying at our home and had come to Michigan early to make sure she was here when the baby was born. She and Scott's father live in Tennessee. During the doctor visit, everything checked out okay and seemed to be progressing normally. Just prior to leaving the office, I mentioned to the doctor that I hadn't felt the baby move much over the previous couple of days. Upon hearing this, my doctor said he wanted me to go to the hospital for a non-stress test, just to be on the safe side. I was unaware of it, but a storm front was moving into our area. It wasn't showing up on my radar yet.

I went to the hospital, along with my mother-in-law, expecting to be sent home in an hour or two. I wasn't really concerned about our baby's lack of movement. I had always heard that babies don't move as much prior to delivery. Being my first full-term pregnancy, I didn't know what to feel or expect. My due-date was only a week and two days away. I thought our baby might be just as eager to meet us as we were to meet him or her and, therefore, come early.

During the test, our baby's heart rate was decelerating during my contractions. I had been experiencing mild contractions for weeks. I began to get a little concerned during the test when the nurse asked me to put on an oxygen mask. When Scott's mom came into the room and saw me with the mask on, I could tell from the look on her face that she was also concerned. Still believing they had me on oxygen "just to be on the safe side," I downplayed the situation to her, not wanting her to be unduly nervous. After the nurse consulted with my doctor over the phone, it was decided that it would be best to induce labor, since I was so near my due date. I had the nurse leave a message for Scott at work (this was before the days of widespread cell phone use), and I was on my way to the birthing suite. Clouds had begun to move into the area, but I had no idea what was coming.

After I was admitted to the hospital and prepared for delivery, an obstetrical resident broke my water and discovered it was meconium-stained. I had just resigned from a full-time registered nursing position at this same hospital the week prior. It was my strong desire to stay at home with my new baby and devote myself to becoming the best mother I could be for him or her. As a result of my nursing training, I knew that meconium-stained amniotic fluid meant that our baby suffered from hypoxia (a low oxygen level) while still in my womb. Normally, placental fluid is clear, but our baby's was green.

Scott had arrived just prior to this and was asked to change into hospital surgical scrubs "just in case" I needed to have a Caesarean section. The clouds were visible now, but not threatening. Things wouldn't be picture perfect, but that was okay. While still a student, I had cared for babies whose amniotic fluid had been meconium-stained. Each of those babies was discharged from the hospital without any serious complications. They may have had an infection, but those things could be easily remedied with antibiotics.

Seeing the color of my water, the doctors decided to test our baby's scalp pH and warned me that if it were below a certain number, I would need a C-section. The results were back in just a couple of minutes and as soon as they discovered the result, I was RUSHED to the operating room, where Scott sat outside the door and waited, not permitted to come in. As a nurse myself, I knew that the situation was not good when everyone began calling out orders "STAT!" and scurrying around.

I can still see the scene in my mind today. The doctor who would perform the surgery was on my right side telling the nurse,

"Splash and go!"

The anesthesiologist was on my left. Nurses were rushing about preparing not only me but also the room. My own doctor couldn't make it in time. Everything happened so fast. It would have comforted me to see him. I knew "splash and go" meant "give her a quick swipe and I'll start cutting," which reinforced the gravity of the situation to me.

The clouds were now looming large, gray, and about to burst. I was really scared at that point and I laid on the table praying for our child's safety. The clock in the operating room read 6:11 p.m. I was quickly put to sleep.

When I awoke, I was told that our baby was a boy, born just 10 minutes after I had last glimpsed the time on the clock. Bradley Scott Wanamaker – 6 pounds, 8 ounces. Scott was told that Bradley was "tired" and needed to be taken to the Neonatal Intensive Care Unit (NICU), where my sister-in-law, Tracy, worked as a nurse. Tracy told me months later that when he was born, he wasn't breathing on his own and needed to be re-suscitated. We, of course, didn't know this at the time and were extremely excited. The moment we had waited nine months for had finally arrived. Scott was able to see Bradley shortly after he was born, but I couldn't see him for a few hours, because I had to wait for the anesthesia to wear off. What I thought was an impending cloud burst seemingly turned out to be nothing. It blew quickly past us, leaving me to believe everything would be fine in a few days. We would soon be home enjoying our newborn son. Or so I thought.

The first time I saw him was almost unbelievable. One minute I was pregnant and about to be put to sleep, and the next, I woke up and had a baby. It was almost hard to believe he was MY son. Yet, there he was. Beautiful blond hair and blue, blue eyes. I surveyed every inch of him. Yep, ten fingers and ten toes. Even fuzzy hair on his shoulders. I savored every perfect part. Initially, he was under an oxygen hood with only one IV and sucking on a hospital-issue green pacifier. One of the doctors quipped that he was the only natural blond in the NICU. We didn't know at the time, but we found out about 3 months later that he has albinism, a genetic disorder that causes severe visual impairment and significantly increases the risk of developing skin cancer. We did notice that, instead of focusing on anything, Bradley's eyes scanned back and forth (a condition called nystagmus). I don't know why, but we didn't think much about it. God only gives us what we can deal with at the time. He knew what we would be facing in just a matter of hours. We were blissfully ignorant.

At the time, I thought he needed the IV and oxygen because he possibly had an infection from the meconium staining. I wanted to hold him but was told by the nurses that he was just too tired. Scott and I returned to the birthing suite to get some sleep after seeing Bradley for the first time. After all, we were new parents. We should get as much sleep as possible while we were still able to do so, before the demands of a newborn at home would interrupt our sleep patterns.

After having slept for a few hours in the birthing suite, we were awakened early in the morning, shortly after 1 o'clock, by a resident physician who told us that Bradley had begun having seizures. I don't remember what else she said (my mind was still foggy from the anesthesia), but after she left I began to cry and desperately wanted to go see him. I knew I wouldn't be able to get into the NICU to see him with so much happening, so eventually, somehow, I fell back asleep. Clouds had reappeared, and it began to rain.

After receiving permission from the NICU staff, we went to see him later that morning. We were surprised to find him on a ventilator with numerous IV's, catheters, monitors and everything else necessary to sustain him. The days and weeks that followed were extremely difficult. His platelet levels were below the critical level, and he required platelet transfusions. I was asked by the neonatal physicians to be temporarily discharged from the hospital so I could be taken to the American Red Cross headquarters in Detroit to donate my platelets for him. Even though this was highly unusual, they felt strongly that my platelets would be best for him. His body would be less likely to reject them in a transfusion.

His kidneys had begun to shut down, his heart was enlarged, and doctors feared that part of his bowel may have begun to die. My sister-in-law later confided that, at the time, his condition was the most critical of all the babies in the NICU. He underwent a multitude of tests, including testing for rare diseases, to try to determine what was causing his seizures.

The worst day of my life was the day I learned the results from an MRI done on Bradley in the hours following his seizures. It was morning; he was two days old; and Scott's mom was in the room with him and seven or eight other babies. I went to go pump my milk in a small, enclosed room within the NICU. The milk would be frozen and stored to be fed to him at a later time. After I finished pumping, one of his many doctors lightly knocked on the door and asked to come in and speak with me. He proceeded to tell me that the MRI revealed hemorrhaging in Bradley's brain. He went on to say that this bleeding could cause cerebral palsy and other related difficulties. After the doctor left the room, I sat there alone. I struggled to absorb what I had just heard. I sat staring at the wall and yet stared at nothing in particular. My head was spinning with the enormity of it all. I was stunned and completely devastated. This was life-altering, potentially marriage-shaking news. I could hardly speak without crying. I had a continuous lump in my throat all day long. I dreaded telling Scott. I couldn't bear to tell his mom. I asked my sister-in-law to do it. I knew what this news could mean. The storm that had seemed to pass had now turned into a tempest with stinging, pouring rain and heavy winds.

Chapter 2 – In *All* Things?

And we know that God causes all things to work together for good to those who love God, to those who are called according to His purpose (Romans 8:28).

That well-known verse from the Bible is often quoted, but do we really believe what it says? Do we really think God is able to work through every single situation in our lives for our good? That verse doesn't say that all things *are* good, but God can indeed bring good from a horrible, heartbreaking event.

Over the course of Bradley's first few months we learned, with much relief, that the enlargement of his heart was a temporary effect of the lack of oxygen in his brain. I took him weekly for blood tests which determined that his kidney function had returned to normal. His platelet levels also began to rise steadily, after being stabilized during his hospital stay. Scott and I were hopeful that he would continue on to what is considered "normal" infant development. After all, I consoled myself, if he did suffer the effects of cerebral palsy, the spectrum of disability can vary widely. He could grow to have nearly imperceptible deficits. There was also the other end of the spectrum, but I didn't want to think about that. I remained hopeful for the future.

Once home, we settled into a routine and I became absorbed in motherhood. I listened regularly to Christian radio broadcasts in my quest to be the best mother I could be for Bradley. I learned about a wide variety of topics, but I now had a new interest in the programs devoted to stories of people with varying levels of disability. I heard a story of a little boy with cerebral palsy who was about 6 years old at the time. This little boy was talkative and nearly bursting with enthusiasm. I had hope Bradley would one day be like that little boy. I also heard a story of a pastor with cerebral palsy. While his speech was affected by his disability, his mind certainly was not. Not only was his mind sharp, but he was married and had a family of his own. I was encouraged that Bradley, too, could one day grow to manhood, meet a young Christian woman God had selected just for him, and have a family.

Within just a few months, we began to notice that some of the typical milestones of infant development were significantly delayed. Bradley's body was weak all over. He held up his head with great effort and difficulty. He couldn't roll over as most babies do. At seven months of age when compared to his cousin, who is two weeks older than him, there was already an obvious difference in their abilities and degree of emotional attachment. However, even with the delays in his development and struggles, I remained hopeful. There were some things that Bradley could do very well.

It became apparent to us that Bradley loved music. Whenever he heard music, he would stop whatever he was doing and listen. When he was about 9 months old, our church's long-time organist, Frieda, played the piano for him. At the time, Frieda, Scott, and I were among the members of our church's hand bell choir. She remains one of the most musically gifted people I have ever known. During our bell choir rehearsals her keenly tuned ear picked up the slightest error.

"Who's playing B-flat? It's supposed to be B-natural."

The rest of us looked at each other in disbelief. How could she identify a single wrong note among a whole chorus of other notes being played simultaneously? During one of our rehearsals, we were together with a small group of people in our church's choir room. We had previously shared with Frieda how much Bradley loved music. She gently took him in her arms, sat down at the piano with him on her lap, and played for him. He was mesmerized by her playing. He didn't reach out to touch the keys as many babies would have done. He just listened intently to her playing. His enjoyment filled her with delight.

Bradley also loved to have songs sung to him. Later, when he began to talk (when I say talk, I mean repeating words or phrases after us), he loved to sing. His vocal pitch was perfect. Scott and I marveled because he seemed to remember every song he had ever heard. He probably knew over one hundred songs! His beautiful singing later became a ministry to me.

Scott and I also noticed Bradley's phenomenal memory. We had a set of flashcards with different objects pictured on each card. The set contained probably 50 cards. In addition to doing the usual toddler things like reciting the alphabet and counting to ten, he was able to identify every single card when we held it up for him to see. It was clear to us at this point that Bradley had significant visual impairment. He was able to see objects close to him, but we weren't sure how well he could see them or how far he could see.

Bradley loved to have books read to him. It was common for us to sit down with him and read a stack of books. He couldn't carry on a conversation with us, but he was able to memorize his books. He enjoyed sitting on the floor with his books scattered around him. As he turned the pages, he would either identify pictures on them or recite the story from memory. All of these things that Bradley was able to do encouraged us. His development was delayed, but at least he was developing and learning.

I focused on doing what I could to help Bradley develop to his fullest potential. When he was about 6 months old, our doctor suggested regular physical therapy. We began seeing the therapists at a nearby medical center in an effort to strengthen Bradley's neck and back muscles. At home, I was occupied with the exercises suggested by the therapists as well as the usual demands of being a wife and mother. Around this same time, we learned that I was soon to be occupied with the newest addition to our family. We were blessed with Bradley's brother, Kyle, when Bradley was a little over fifteen months old. Looking back now, I believe the Lord brought Kyle when he did, and later, his little sister, Katherine, as a comfort to us through a difficult time.

As time passed, Bradley's developmental delays became more obvious. Later in infancy, when I attempted to introduce solid foods to him, we discovered he had a very difficult time swallowing. He gagged at even the smallest lump in his food. When I say small lump, I mean even smaller than a pea. Every accomplishment he achieved was a struggle. A pediatric specialist suggested we enroll him in an early intervention program to help him in different areas. At the early intervention center, he received physical therapy, occupational therapy, speech therapy, and was seen by a visual services consultant. I took him twice per week. We didn't have any grandparents in the area or extended family available to watch Kyle while I took Bradley to therapy, so Kyle came along, too. It was very difficult taking them both, especially during the colder months. By this time, Bradley was almost two years old and not walking. Kyle, of course, was still too little to walk. Into the center I would trudge with Bradley on one hip while holding Kyle in his infant carrier with the other arm. I'm exhausted just thinking about it today, but the Lord gave me the strength to do it at the time.

When he was around two years old, Bradley began having seizures again. He hadn't experienced a seizure since his hospitalization as a newborn. The first time he had a seizure at home I was terrified. My training as a registered nurse had prepared me for many things, but not for this. Not when it was *my* son. I walked into his room in the morning to get him ready for the day. His eyes were open, but he didn't respond to me. As I tried to get a response from him, I noticed that his lips were a dusky gray color. He appeared not to be breathing. I panicked initially. My mind cried out, *Oh, Jesus, no! Not this! Please don't let my baby die!* I quickly hurried to the phone, called 911, and returned to his side. I attempted to give him CPR. He coughed when I breathed into his lungs, so I figured he was at least breathing a little bit, even though I couldn't see it. An ambulance arrived quickly at our home, and Bradley was whisked away to the nearest hospital. He was admitted to the hospital for several days to stop the seizures and undergo neurological testing. This was the first of his visits to the hospital for seizures.

We had entered a new phase with Bradley. We never knew where or when a seizure would occur. Some seizures are short and need no intervention, but not these. When Bradley had a seizure, it wouldn't stop until he received medication to stop them. At the time, the medication could only be given intravenously. I was always concerned, because an untreated, prolonged seizure could cause further damage to the brain or even death. What if he had one at night while we were sleeping? What if he had one and we were unable to quickly get him to the hospital? We were surprised more than once by a seizure when we were away from home. He had a seizure while Scott was driving home with Kyle after having our car serviced. Another time, he had a seizure while I was driving home from meeting Scott for lunch. Both times we wound up back at the hospital to get the seizure under control. He had seizures at home. He had seizures at church. We just never knew. I had an unspoken fear of the possibility that I could walk into his room one morning and find him dead.

As Bradley further progressed into his toddler years, it was slowly revealed to me that he was going to be at that other end of the spectrum when it came to his level of disability from cerebral palsy. You know – the other end I didn't want to think about earlier.

The programs of the early intervention center I had been taking Bradley to for almost a year and a half ended at age three. A couple months prior to the end of the school year, the center held parent meetings to acquaint parents with the various types of special education schools and programs available to our children. I knew Bradley would need some kind of special education program at this point, but I was in no way prepared for the type of school he would require.

I was advised by the staff at the center which school they thought would be the best fit for Bradley. We were informed of the dates and times for the school's orientation night. Scott and I drove to the meeting unsure of what to expect. As we entered the building, small wheelchairs lined the hallways. We entered a small meeting room with other parents and were introduced to the school's principal, vice principal and psychologist. They began the meeting by welcoming us to the school. They then began explaining the different programs the school offers. The first program they listed was the Educable Mentally Impaired (EMI) program. Next came the Trainable Mentally Impaired (TMI) program. Next was the Severely Mentally Impaired (SMI) program. They introduced the Severely Multiply Impaired (SXI) program last. Bradley was assigned to a Severely

Multiply Impaired classroom. I was crushed. It was degrading and humiliating to hear that the school system didn't consider Bradley to be educable or even trainable. What were these people saying? Didn't they know they were talking about *my* son? Couldn't they find a kinder way to tell me what they thought the scope of his abilities would be? I was completely and utterly devastated. After concluding their presentation, they served refreshments and gave us a tour of the building. I hardly heard a word they said. I felt as though a piece of my heart and my hope had been ripped away. I wanted to run from that place and go somewhere alone and cry. I could not believe the students at this school were his peers and this was the type of school Bradley would be attending.

He began attending his new school in June of 2001. The SXI school program attended year-round. He had a wonderful Christian lady as his teacher. She was amazing! Within a couple months at school, she had him drinking from a straw and feeding himself almost entirely independently with a spoon. These were big steps for him. Prior to this, he drank exclusively from a bottle. He was unable to drink from a cup and didn't have the dexterity to hold eating utensils. With a special spoon, plate, and the constant help of an occupational therapist at school, he made quick progress. He had even begun walking with a walker up and down the hallways at school all by himself!

Not long after these encouraging signs, however, we began to witness a slow and gradual decline in Bradley's ability levels in all areas.

Somewhere during the course of Bradley's first year at his new school, he began having frequent, lengthy crying fits. It is difficult to pinpoint a precise time, because the changes were so gradual. These crying fits didn't seem to have any particular trigger and could last for what seemed to be a very long time. The most disturbing thing about them for me, though, was that I, as Bradley's mother, was unable to console him. I tried to hold him to comfort him, but he pushed me away. He rejected my affection and most of the time didn't want me too near him. He resisted my attempts to cuddle with him. I struggled with this. It was frustrating for me to want to be able to help and console him when he didn't want it. I remember praying and asking the Lord to fill me with love for Bradley, because I could feel myself beginning to harden toward him as a result of what seemed like regular rejection. Thankfully, the Lord did fill me with immeasurable love for my precious son.

By his fourth birthday, Bradley had lost some of the gains he had worked so hard to achieve. He no longer was able to use his walker. We believe he still had the physical ability to use it at the time, but he refused to use it anymore. He no longer worked to feed himself with a spoon. Thankfully, he was still able to use a straw.

Scott and I were most filled with sorrow by the regression in Bradley's ability to communicate. He was never able to communicate normally, but there was a time when he was able to make his desires known to us. After being hospitalized for dehydration resulting from a nasty stomach virus, Bradley was home needing a drink from his bottle. He was scared of it because every time he tried to drink from it before going into the hospital, he got sick. I encouraged him to drink at every opportunity, wishing to avoid a readmission to the hospital. I held his bottle down in front of him and he said,

"No, Momo," (his way of saying Momma) "no want it."

That was a long time ago. He has very little meaningful speech now. He can only communicate by pushing things away that he doesn't want, or reaching for things he does want. He rarely sings anymore. As a result of this regression in his speech, we believe Bradley has autism in addition to his other impairments. While autism cannot be definitively diagnosed because of his brain injury at birth, a specialist told us that kids with brain injuries do not regress behaviorally.

Today, Bradley has many deficits. He is totally dependent upon others for his care. He can't walk but uses a wheelchair. He has muscle contractures in his legs, which have required countless painful injections and which have seriously restricted his leg motion. He continues to need a daily medication to maintain control of his seizures, as well as a sedative to help him sleep at night. He has asthma. He is unable to feed himself independently and has an esophageal condition that at times causes him great discomfort when he eats. He wears diapers. He doesn't meaningfully interact with us or his brother or sister. Unless God miraculously heals him, he will never marry, have children, or speak the words,

"I love you, Momma."

All of this sounds depressing, doesn't it? Thankfully, that is not the end of the story. What a dreary ending that would be! Remember Romans 8:28 from the beginning of this chapter? In *all* things, God is able to work for the good of those who love him. So, what good has God wrought from our experiences with Bradley? Has our suffering had value? Has there been a purpose for this trial? Let's explore these questions in the coming chapters.

Chapter 3 – Broken Dreams

Shout for joy, O heavens! And rejoice, O earth!
Break forth into joyful shouting, O mountains! For
the LORD has comforted His people And will have
compassion on His afflicted (Isaiah 49:13).

At the close of the last chapter, I referenced Romans 8:28, which tells us God is able to work for our good in all things. The implication from this verse is that we will experience hardship, setbacks, and heartache in this world. If only good things happened to us, would God need to work for our good from those already good things? It follows then that our focus should be on the benefit He brings about in spite of our circumstances. From this point, in each chapter I will discuss some of the specific challenges we have faced with Bradley. The challenges, however, will not be the focus. The challenges will only serve to lead to my concluding points. The heart of each chapter, ultimately, will be the blessing God has brought about as a result of our suffering with our son.

I have never experienced sorrow like I experienced during Bradley's younger childhood years. As I watched what abilities he did have disappear, I sank into a pit of despair. I was heart-broken. There were so many things I realized Bradley would never be able to do, unless God intervened. With each milestone of development that his younger brother and, later, his little sister achieved, I was reminded of Bradley's limitations.

When I was in college, I had a friend whose son suffered a profound traumatic brain injury during his teen years. This was before Scott and I had children of our own. Her son was hit by a car while riding his bicycle. Prior to the accident, he was a sharp-minded, perfectly able-bodied young man. As a result of his accident, he was left significantly impaired. He lost many of the abilities he had prior to his accident. Tasks that were easily completed before the accident became a challenge. I remember something my friend said to me about how difficult it was for her to adapt to her son's new level of functioning. She said,

"It's not just one loss; it's a series of losses."

I didn't fully understand what she meant until I went through the grieving process myself. Although I didn't realize it at the time, I was grieving the death of our dreams for our son. Bradley had not died, thankfully, but I grieved for all that should have been. I grieved for all the achievements of "normal" human development. His first steps, potty training (yes, even that), his first day of school, first baseball game. The list goes on – his high school and college graduations, marriage, and even grandchildren. Every milestone Kyle and Katherine accomplished accentuated Bradley's losses for me. One of the most difficult things a parent can face is to see his or her child struggle and be absolutely powerless and helpless to change the situation.

Try to change the situation we did! We prayed countless times asking the Lord to heal Bradley. Family members prayed for him. Friends prayed for him. People at our church prayed for him. I reminded God of what He said regarding healing in His word. I reminded Him that He said in both the Old and New Testaments that by His wounds we are healed.

"Lord, you said that you are the God who heals all our diseases. You said that if we have faith as small as a mustard seed, we could tell a mountain to move and it would! You said that if we ask anything in your name, you would do it. Please, God, *please* heal my son."

I tried to convince the Lord that Bradley's healing would be a good move to advance His Kingdom. "Lord, just think of how many people might turn to you if you completely healed Bradley. It would be in the newspapers! It would be on TV! People would see your power and turn to you."

I was gently reminded of the incidences in Scripture where people witnessed first-hand Jesus' miraculous healings. While some people did turn to the Lord after witnessing these miracles, many of them did not. I was forgetting the example Jesus gave us when he prayed in the Garden of Gethsemane. Knowing the intense suffering that lay ahead of him, Jesus fell to the ground and prayed,

> "My Father, if it is possible, let this cup pass from Me; *yet not as I will, but as You will.*" (Matthew 26:39, emphasis mine).

At this point, I feel it is necessary to mention some views on sickness and healing prevalent in the Christian world today, often called the Faith Movement. The primary focus of these teachings is physical healing, not spiritual healing and growth. As I noted in the Foreword, there are influential teachers who misrepresent the truth of Scripture. They claim that a Christian's life should be free from difficulty and full of the blessings of our choosing. In the most extreme examples, believers are taught that Christians should never be sick. It is also taught that it is *always* God's will to heal us. Is that what Scripture teaches? In John 16:33, Jesus states,

> "In this world *you will have* trouble. But, take heart! I have overcome the world" (NIV; emphasis mine).

Our Lord tells us clearly that we will face difficulty. James 1:2-3 (NIV) says,

> Consider it pure joy, my brothers, whenever you face *trials of many kinds*, because you know that the testing of your faith produces perseverance (emphasis mine).

Now we are assured that our troubles won't be isolated, one-time occurrences. In addition to telling us without question that our lives will not be without difficulty, these verses also give us hope. We know from the verse in James that there is a purpose for the suffering we experience. Our heartaches are not pointless! Trials develop godly character in our lives. God promises He will never leave us nor forsake us! Jesus sent the Holy Spirit to comfort, guide, encourage, and strengthen us along the way. Whatever situation we find ourselves in, He is right there to help us!

I mention these teachings because Scott and I have been personally affected by them. The teachers within the faith movement place a burden on those who are suffering that our Heavenly Father never intended. They imply the reason God doesn't heal you or your loved one is due to your lack of faith. You are left to wonder, *If I just had more faith, would God heal me or my loved one?*

When Bradley was very young, Scott and I were told by a well-intentioned individual that Bradley was healed of his seizures. This person believed that if he confessed that Bradley would be healed, *and we, as Bradley's parents, had faith to believe it*, it would come to pass. There was only one problem. Bradley wasn't healed. He continued to have seizures following this proclamation of faith. To follow the logic, if God said he was going to heal Bradley (providing we had enough faith to believe for this miracle) and he wasn't healed, it was our fault. It was implied that our lack of faith stood in the way of a supernatural move of God.

Another time, we were invited at the last minute to a special healing service at a nearby church. The visiting speaker was a man reputed to have a special healing ability from God. We declined the invitation due to a prior commitment. I didn't have a desire to go anyway. In my discouragement, I didn't want to be disappointed if another prayer for healing seemed to fall on deaf ears. I was comforted as I recalled the story of the centurion in Matthew 8:5-8:

> And when Jesus entered Capernaum, a centurion came to Him, imploring Him, and saying, "Lord, my servant is lying paralyzed at home, fearfully tormented." Jesus said to him, "I will come and heal him." But the centurion said, "Lord, I am not worthy for You to come under my roof, but just say the word, and my servant will be healed."

If it were God's will to heal Bradley, Scott and I wouldn't have to take him to a special location at a special time to see a special speaker. God could do it anywhere and at any time. Let me say emphatically that I believe with all my heart that the Lord has the power to completely heal Bradley with a single command. One word from God would change Bradley's life (and ours) in an instant, but that healing word hasn't come. Not yet, anyway.

It isn't always God's will to heal us on this side of eternity. The saints of God have suffered throughout history. Some were healed and restored. In one of the most familiar examples of suffering in the Bible, Job is healed and restored at the end of the book. However, some of the effects of Job's suffering were irreversible. Although the Lord did bless Job with more children following his restoration, the children he had prior to his test remained dead. Some saints of God were not healed and continued to suffer. Some were martyred. In His infinite, unfathomable wisdom, God chose not to intervene. People continue to suffer and die today. We live in a fallen world marred by sin and death. Until we are taken home to be with our Lord or until He returns, we should not be surprised by difficulty in our lives.

I am certainly not encouraging people to give up praying for their healing or the healing of a loved one. Jesus admonished us in the parable of the persistent widow to always pray and never give up. The key to the prayer of Jesus in Matthew 26:39 above is submission. We must submit our will to the perfect will of our Father, even in the midst of circumstances we don't understand. God doesn't just want us to submit to Him, though, out of duty. He desires for us to know him. He wants us to have an intimate relationship with Him.

As I began to realize that Bradley might not be healed any time soon, I was filled with sadness. I cried a lot. When we were at church, I would often fight back tears throughout the worship service, especially during hymns like "Great is Thy Faithfulness." Every time the chorus of voices would crescendo to "Strength for today and bright hope for tomorrow," I was moved to tears. I desperately needed strength for each day and I clung to the bright hope for tomorrow.

I felt isolated and very alone. I felt like a stranger in my own church and that no one could relate to me. No one I knew had a child just like Bradley. Certainly there were no other children at our church like him. As can be expected, many people didn't know how to respond to us. I could tell they were curious about Bradley, but were afraid to ask us questions about him for fear of saying the wrong thing. Other people were clearly uncomfortable around him, which was very upsetting to me.

I struggled with all of the "why" questions. At times, I railed against God in anger. *Why **my** son, Lord? Why him and not me? Why my family? Why does everything have to be such a struggle for Bradley, Lord? I see other families whose children* *are completely healthy. They don't have to face the things we deal with. Why, God?*

As Bradley grew older and his care required more and more of our time and energy, we were unable to do many of the things families often take for granted. *Why can't we do those things, Lord? Why can't we just go out to eat when we want without creating a scene? Why can't we go on a vacation like this or that family has done? I don't like this at all, Lord!* It all seemed unfair to me and was not what I had envisioned for my family. Thankfully, God was compassionate and understood my pity parties and even my mini-tantrums.

Eventually, there were important benefits to all those feelings of sadness, despair, and anguish. Feeling alone drove me to my Heavenly Father. Only He could know and truly understand the pain I was experiencing. Only He could listen to my seemingly endless sobs with compassion and tenderness. Only He could begin to heal my broken heart. In the midst of my pain and loneliness, the Lord was beginning to weave blessing from my suffering. How could I ever have known the richness of His comforting presence without a need for comfort? To need comfort is to have known discouragement and heartbreak. Ultimately, viewed in this light, our pain can be seen as being good. It drives us to the only One who can satisfy every need and hunger of the human soul.

I sought the Scriptures for comfort and hope. I was drawn closer to the Lord through the study of His Word and through prayer. His Word came alive to me like never before and comforted me like nothing else could. I saw His tenderness when I read in Psalm 34:18 that the Lord is close to the brokenhearted and saves those who are crushed in spirit. I was reminded in Psalm 147:3 that, though intensely painful at the time, my heartbreak would be mended. Even though I felt alone, Psalm 46:1 assured me that I was not. I have listed these comforting Scriptures, and others that encouraged me in my sorrow, below. Experiencing the intimate comfort of my Heavenly Father and being drawn closer to Him were the first ways He began to work *in all things* for my good.

Scriptures for Comfort:

Psalm 34:18- The LORD is near to the brokenhearted And saves those who are crushed in spirit.

Psalm 147:3- He heals the brokenhearted And binds up their wounds.

Psalm 46:1- God is our refuge and strength, A very present help in trouble.

Psalm 51:17- The sacrifices of God are a broken spirit; A broken and a contrite heart, O God, You will not despise.

Isaiah 40:11- Like a shepherd He will tend His flock, In His arm He will gather the lambs And carry them in His bosom; He will gently lead the nursing ewes.

Matthew 5:4- Blessed are those who mourn, for they shall be comforted.

Isaiah 51:12- I, even I, am He who comforts you....

Isaiah 66:13- As one whom his mother comforts, so I will comfort you....

2 Corinthians 1:3-4- Blessed be the God and Father of our Lord Jesus Christ, the Father of mercies and God of all comfort, who comforts us in all our affliction so that we will be able to comfort those who are in any affliction with the comfort with which we ourselves are comforted by God.

Isaiah 49:13- Shout for joy, O heavens! And rejoice, O earth! Break forth into joyful shouting, O mountains! For the LORD has comforted His people And will have compassion on His afflicted.

Isaiah 33:2- O Lord, be gracious to us; we have waited for you. Be their strength every morning, Our salvation also in the time of distress.

Isaiah 43:1-2- Do not fear, for I have redeemed you; I have called you by name; you are Mine! When you pass through the waters, I will be with you; And through the rivers, they will not overflow you. When you walk through the fire, you will not be scorched, Nor will the flame burn you.

Chapter 4 – I Trust You, Lord. No, *Really*, I Do!

> Trust in the LORD with all your heart And do not lean on your own understanding. In all your ways acknowledge Him, And He will make your paths straight. (Proverbs 3:5-6).

In a healthy relationship between a parent and child, a child completely trusts his or her parents without hesitation from an early age. Within the context of a loving environment, a child recognizes his needs will be met. In infancy, every need of a baby must be met by his parents. During the exciting toddler years, a child still looks to his parents for his basic needs. At this age, a child also looks for reassurance. When in an unfamiliar or frightening situation, a child finds solace in the presence of his mother or father. A smile from momma or daddy encourages a child to explore, attempt new skills, and learn about his environment. In the later years of school and adolescence, a child depends on the guidance, support, approval, and comfort of his parents. Undergirding all of this is a foundation of trust.

Although we as parents make mistakes, if we provide a loving, peaceful, nurturing environment for our children, we will likely be the recipients of our child's trust. Our children will continue to trust us unless we act in a manner which causes them to doubt our trustworthiness. This mirrors, though imperfectly, the trust we have as believers in our Heavenly Father. We try our best as Christian parents to train up our children to follow the Lord. We should strive to live as examples in our words and through our actions, but we will, at multiple points, fail them. We might unintentionally say something hurtful to our son or daughter. We might not recognize an emotional need in his life and neglect to spend needed time with him. She may see us treat another person unkindly or disrespectfully. The list goes on and on. The point is that we *will* fail them. We are imperfect people.

Contrast that with our Heavenly Father, who is perfect in every way. He is all-knowing. He knows what His children are feeling and thinking at all times. He is all-powerful and limitless. The events of the world are in His capable hands. He never makes mistakes. He has never failed us and He never will. Knowing and having faith in His attributes should make it easy for us to trust Him.

It is easy to say you trust God when everything is going your way. Then something unexpected comes along that is outside of your control. Call it a storm, a trial, or being thrown one of life's "curve balls." This "something" will differ from person to person. Our circumstances are as uniquely designed by God as we were uniquely knit together in the wombs of our mothers. Whatever your "something" is, it threatens you. Disease, divorce, death, disability, etc. It doesn't matter what it's called. What matters is the effect the circumstance has on you. It destroys the comfortable place you were in. It makes you uneasy and scared. Questions creep into your mind. If left unanswered with the truth of Scripture, these questions can grow into doubt.

My "something" was Bradley and his future, as well as ours. When I realized that our future would not be what I had envisioned for my family, I was filled with many questions. The severity of Bradley's disability caused uncertainty for all of us. At first, my questions focused on the near-term. He was scheduled to start riding a bus to school when he was only three years old. How could I trust the bus driver, a total stranger? Bradley is defenseless and, as a result, extremely vulnerable. What if the person was abusive to him? He would never be able to communicate abuse or mistreatment. What about his teacher and his therapists? I would be entrusting my precious boy to them for nearly seven hours each day. What if they hurt him? When he began having crying fits, I wondered if the screaming and crying would strain their patience beyond limits. I knew he would be at the mercy of those entrusted with his care.

As Kyle and Katherine grew older, I wondered what effect our situation would have on them. How would they react? Would they be embarrassed by their brother? When Bradley's behavioral difficulties became an issue, I questioned how they would be affected by missing out on different activities. Would they resent having Bradley for a brother? Would they resent us for not finding a way to do things we were unable to do?

What about my marriage? Our situation was not what Scott and I had expected from married life. We weren't expecting perfection, but we planned for a life of relative ease. We were both college graduates and looked forward to watching our family grow and experiencing some of the good things of life. I had read that the divorce rate for couples with a disabled child was 80%. That statistic frightened me. I had also heard that a husband and wife should have regular "date nights." How would it be possible to feed and nurture our marital relation-ship? We couldn't go out on regular dates. We were fortunate if we could arrange to go out twice per year! Would we grow apart? We were both grieving and generally avoided talking about it. We knew if we really talked about what was going on, we might both dissolve into sobbing heaps.

As if all these questions weren't enough, I had more questions about our future. At the time, I was able to carry Bradley and take care of his physical needs. But, kids grow. How would I care for Bradley when he became too big for me to carry? How would my body hold up to the increasing physical strain? As I've related before, his behavior was challenging at times. What if his behavior became too aggressive for us to manage? What about after he finished his school program? What then? What would we do for his living arrangements? Would he continue to live with us? Who would care for him after Scott and I are gone? My questions were endless. I didn't have answers to any of them and I didn't like it. The situations represented by my questions were completely outside of my control. If you were to have asked me at that time if I trusted God, I would have answered,

"Absolutely!" But did I *really*?

A few years ago, our family became eligible to receive respite care services. These services provide temporary relief, or respite, for families from their caregiving responsibilities. Receiving the respite services was unexpected, but welcome, news. We had applied for assistance the previous two years and had been denied. We finally qualified when Scott unexpectedly lost his job. Only seven weeks later, Scott had a new job and we quickly recognized that his job loss was another way the Lord worked *in all things* for our good. In addition to having a respite worker come into our home to help provide care for Bradley, he was now able to stay at a respite home for children in our area. His stay at the respite home could vary in length. It could be an overnight stay, a weekend stay, or an entire week, depending on our family's needs. With this news, we would now be able to plan our first real family vacation.

Scott and I decided to take Kyle and Katherine to Disney World. I had mixed emotions. While I was excited that we were finally going on a big vacation with Kyle and Katherine, I was also saddened by the fact that Bradley wouldn't be going along as well. When our children were younger, Scott and I planned that Bradley wouldn't be treated any differently than Kyle or Katherine just because he was limited in his abilities. We planned to do everything together as a family. As time passed, although we desired to have Bradley with us, it wasn't necessarily beneficial for him or us.

We knew it would be better for our whole family for Bradley to stay at the respite home while we were away on vacation. He would prefer the routine of his school schedule to sitting all day in his wheelchair in the hot Florida sun. Furthermore, Kyle and Katherine would have our undivided attention for a whole week, and we would finally have the time to enjoy some much-needed rest.

Overriding these benefits, though, were familiar questions. How could I trust these people I didn't know to care for my son? Not only that, what if one of the other children staying at the home harmed him? What would they do if he had a seizure? What if he got sick while there? Who would take care of him? I was grateful that we were finally able to go on a vacation, but I was also fearful.

I was informed of the process of introducing a child to the respite home by the respite home coordinator. Initially, I was scheduled to take Bradley to the home for a meeting with the home's manager and respite home coordinator. This meeting would be an opportunity for the staff to interview me about Bradley and briefly become acquainted with him. The getting-to-know-Bradley meeting would be followed by a dinner visit. If the dinner visit was successful and there weren't any problems, a weekend visit would be scheduled. If the weekend visit went without difficulty, we would be free to schedule our vacation.

The initial meeting did not go well for me. I didn't know what to expect, since I had never been to a respite home. The respite home's manager answered the door. She asked me to come in, but there was no smile of welcome, nor any attempt at reassurance. She abruptly told me the coordinator hadn't arrived yet. I waited in the foyer, scanning what I could see of the home. The environment seemed sterile. After an awkward minute or two, the coordinator arrived at the front door. She matter-of-factly introduced herself to me and said we could go into the kitchen for our meeting. Again, there was no smile of welcome. The three of us sat at the table while I was peppered with questions about Bradley. What food does he like and dislike? What is his normal daily routine? What does he enjoy doing? The tone was very cold and businesslike. I realized that the information they were collecting was necessary and useful, but at that visit I needed compassion and reassurance. I needed to know that my son would be okay if left at this place. Not just okay, I wanted to know someone would *really* care for him. I felt the familiar lump rising in my throat. I was sure I was going to break down and cry right there in front of those women. Somehow I held it together. The meeting lasted for nearly an hour and concluded with a tour of the home. Thankfully, it was a worker at the home who gave me the tour. Her eyes were warm and smiling. She gave me a small glimmer of hope. Still, I was filled with sadness and sobbed the whole twenty-five minute ride home.

The following week, we were scheduled to go for our dinner visit. I dreaded it. I tried to reassure myself that maybe our first meeting caught both of these ladies on a bad day. Maybe I was being too sensitive. I thought about the previous visit all day. In my mind I kept replaying the scenes of the last meeting. I knew, though, that I needed to get acclimated to the idea of leaving Bradley there for a week. Our vacation depended on it. Yet I knew I could never leave him there if I didn't feel good about it. That afternoon, Bradley ministered to me through his singing. Just a couple hours before we were scheduled to be at the respite home, he began singing a song he has known for years. He first heard the song when he was a toddler, on a compact disc of Christian songs for kids. When Bradley speaks, which isn't often, his words are barely discernible for others. But I recognized the tune immediately and recalled the words of the song. They were, "My heart is ready to trust you, Lord. I trust you know my heart." With those words, I knew the Lord was mindful of exactly how I felt. He understood my concerns and He knew my fears. He was asking me to trust Him. I felt a little like Peter when he was questioned by Jesus about his love for Him. Only in my case, I was being questioned about trust. I felt like He was saying,

"Heather, do you trust me?"

"Yes, Lord, of course, I do." I replied.

Again, "Heather, do you really trust me?"

"Yes, Lord. You know I do."

"Do you trust that I love Bradley more than you do? Do you trust Me to care for him? Do you trust Me to nurture him? Do you trust Me to protect him while you're away?"

In addition to these immediate questions, I felt He was asking me questions about our future.

"Do you trust My wisdom and knowledge? Do you trust My plans for your family?"

I again sought Scripture for comfort and encouragement. One doesn't have to search long to find examples of God's love, protection, and provision for His people. The Old Testament recounts story after story. With each account, we are encouraged that God is indeed who He says He is! He told Noah to anticipate a flood and build an ark. Do you think Noah had any questions for God? He had never even seen rain! God told Abraham to leave the land of his fathers. He promised Abraham He would bless him and make him into a great nation. Since Sarah was barren, do you think Abraham questioned God? What about Joseph? Do you think Joseph ever questioned God's plans when he sat in prison having been falsely accused of a crime? Moses? Moses questioned God. How can I go to Pharaoh? How can I lead over a million people from Egypt? What about the Red Sea, Lord? The list goes on. David. Can you protect me, Lord, from Saul? He's trying to kill me. Ruth. Can you take care of my needs now, Lord? My husband and father-in-law have both died, and I am a foreigner in a strange land.

My point is that God keeps His word. With each promise of Scripture, we can be encouraged that when He says He will do something, He will do it! He is trustworthy! We need not be fearful now or in the future. Certainly, we need to exercise due diligence in selecting caregivers for our loved ones and intervene if there is a concern. We must use discernment and allow the Holy Spirit to guide us. However, there comes a point when we have to trust God. We cannot always be with our loved one. God is *always* with them. Just as He has promised, He will never leave us nor forsake us, and that includes our loved ones.

Our dinner visit at the respite home went well. I was buoyed with confidence in our Lord's promises. I was also encouraged that evening by meeting some of the respite workers who would be caring for Bradley. The same lady that initially gave me hope was there, as well as some other ladies. They seemed caring and I was comforted by their warm demeanor. The dinner visit gave me the reassurance I needed to go ahead with the weekend visit and, later, an entire week.

Three years have passed since our vacation. Bradley did well at the respite home, and the time with Kyle and Katherine was a wonderful blessing for us. In both the weekend and vacation stays, the Lord protected Bradley and kept him healthy while we were away. In addition to that, we saw evidence of the workers' care and thoughtfulness toward Bradley. Both instances when I came to bring him home from respite, I discovered with surprise that they had bought Bradley little gifts to take home with him.

With the assurance that our Lord is trustworthy, loving, and capable comes peace. God orders our steps and makes provision for us each leg of our journey. When we need comfort, He lovingly gives it. When we need reassurance, He graciously gives it. When we need strength, He gives it liberally. Jesus instructs us in Matthew 6:34, "So do not worry about tomorrow; for tomorrow will care for itself. Each day has enough trouble of its own." He knew that our minds could be misdirected to focus on our circumstances and potential problems of the future. We are admonished in Proverbs 3:5 not to lean on our own understanding. Our finite minds will not understand everything that happens to us. We don't have to understand. All we need to do is trust the One who does understand. We need to keep our focus on Him. He is working out His divine plan in each of our lives. He has our best interest in mind. He is able to do exceedingly, abundantly above all that we could ask or think.

Through our respite home experience, and many other situations as well, the Lord has built my trust in Him. He has proven Himself faithful, again and again. He is *more* than worthy of our trust!

Scriptures Encouraging Trust & Peace:

Psalm 20:7- Some boast in chariots and some in horses, But we will boast in the name of the LORD, our God.

Psalm 136:1- Give thanks to the LORD, for He is good, For His lovingkindness is everlasting.

John 14:1- Do not let your heart be troubled; believe in God, believe also in Me.

Isaiah 25:9- And it will be said in that day, 'Behold, this is our God for whom we have waited that He might save us. This is the LORD for whom we have waited; Let us rejoice and be glad in His salvation.'

Psalm 32:10- Many are the sorrows of the wicked, But he who trusts in the LORD, lovingkindness shall surround him.

Jeremiah 29:11- 'For I know the plans that I have for you,' declares the LORD, 'plans for welfare and not for calamity to give you a future and a hope.'

Isaiah 26:3-4- The steadfast of mind You will keep in perfect peace, Because he trusts in You. Trust in the LORD forever, For in GOD the LORD, we have an everlasting Rock.

Isaiah 41:10- 'Do not fear, for I am with you; Do not anxiously look about you, for I am your God. I will strengthen you, surely I will help you, Surely I will uphold you with My righteous right hand.'

Ephesians 3:16- ...that He would grant you, according to the riches of His glory, to be strengthened with power through His Spirit in the inner man....

Philippians 4:6-7- Be anxious for nothing, but in everything by prayer and supplication with thanksgiving let your requests be made known to God. And the peace of God, which surpasses all comprehension, will guard your hearts and your minds in Christ Jesus.

Isaiah 40:11- Like a shepherd He will tend His flock, In His arm He will gather the lambs And carry them in His bosom; He will gently lead the nursing ewes.

1 Timothy 1:12- I thank Christ Jesus our Lord, who has strengthened me, because He considered me faithful, putting me into service....

Psalm 56:3- When I am afraid, I will put my trust in You.

1 Peter 5:7- ...casting all your anxiety on Him, because He cares for you.

Nahum 1:7- The LORD is good, A stronghold in the day of trouble, And He knows those who take refuge in Him.

Ephesians 3:20-21- Now to Him who is able to do far more abundantly beyond all that we ask or think, according to the power that works within us, to Him be the glory in the church and in Christ Jesus to all generations forever and ever. Amen.

Isaiah 43:1-2- Do not fear, for I have redeemed you; I have called you by name; you are Mine! When you pass through the waters, I will be with you; And through the rivers, they will not overflow you. When you walk through the fire, you will not be scorched, Nor will the flame burn you.

Chapter 5 – How long, Lord?!

> For this reason also, since the day we heard of it, we have not ceased to pray for you and to ask that you may be filled with the knowledge of His will in all spiritual wisdom and understanding, so that you will walk in a manner worthy of the Lord, to please Him in all respects, bearing fruit in every good work and increasing in the knowledge of God; strengthened with all power, according to His glorious might, for the attaining of all steadfastness and patience; joyously giving thanks to the Father, who has qualified us to share in the inheritance of the saints in Light (Colossians 1:9-12).

I have never run a marathon. Before undertaking such a challenge, I imagine a runner is filled with energy and excitement. He has trained months for this day. He anticipates that after hours of non-stop running, he will be welcomed across the finish line to the music of cheers and shouts of family and onlookers.

The starting gun pops and he takes his place among the mass moving away from the starting line. A mile or so into the race, the runner settles into a comfortable pace. *I feel good. I can do this*, he thinks. He runs a few miles. He begins to feel less energetic than he felt at the starting line, but he still feels good. He continues to run. Several miles later he not only is feeling less energetic than he was, but he is beginning to feel weary. He still runs.

Now with the race over halfway complete, he has crossed a mental hurdle. *I'm over halfway there. I'm going to do this.* Only a few miles later, he begins to experience fatigue. He is dripping with sweat. Another mile and his body is aching and crying out for rest. It is being strained to its limits. He begins to doubt and question, but he pushes on.

Put one foot in front of the other. Just keep going. He runs on. His pace has slowed, but he still runs. Mile after exhausting mile he runs. Finally, in the distance he faintly sees the finish line. It seems still a long way off, but the sight of it gives him a boost of energy and his pace quickens a bit. He strains, pushes himself, and keeps going.

One-half mile to go. One hundred yards to go. Fifty yards to go, ten. He staggers across the finish line. The grueling race has depleted every reserve of energy his body had within him. He collapses on the ground utterly exhausted. With their happy faces, the cheering people at the finish line admire the runner's efforts and dedication in finishing the race. He is filled with relief and pleased that he was able to accomplish his goal.

At times, I have felt like I'm running a marathon of a different sort. Typically, I'm a pretty laid back and easy-going person and I have always thought myself to be quite patient. I came to realize, however, through our difficulties with Bradley, that my patience had never really been tested. Sure, I had experienced frustration and irritation, but I didn't face it regularly and to any great extent. How can a person claim to be patient if they haven't been tested in a significant difficulty? In our culture of instant gratification, it is hard for us to wait for anything. How can we have patience if we've never had to wait for an answer to prayer?

I mentioned briefly in Chapter 2 that Bradley began having crying fits when he was younger in which he would become inconsolable. These episodes were unpredictable and seemed to last a very long time. I repeatedly attempted to comfort him, but he would just push me away. Once I was satisfied his physical needs were met (not hungry, wet, or in pain), the only solution left for me was to put him in his bedroom until he calmed down. I tried to go somewhere in our house where his crying and screaming wouldn't seem so loud, but I couldn't escape it. I could hear it in every room of our house. Some days, the stress of these fits was nearly unbearable. I was immensely frustrated and at times even literally banged my head on the wall in an attempt to release some of my frustration. I didn't know what to do. Nothing I did for him stopped the fits. He just had to cry them out. It was draining mentally.

Thankfully, the frequency of these episodes has diminished considerably with age, to where now they are almost non-existent. This is only one of the behavioral challenges that we've had to face.

When Bradley was around three or four years of age, he began what is referred to as self-stimulating behavior. I learned from Bradley's neurologist that this is common for children with brain injuries. A child may rock back and forth constantly, bite himself repeatedly, or bang his head on things. Children who engage in these behaviors are providing a stimulus to their brains, albeit painful ones, in place of normal brain activity. These children may be blind or deaf. They may not be able to read or explore things as other children do. The self-stimulating behaviors replace these normal brain-stimulating activities.

Bradley's first self-stimulating behavior was biting himself. When he was frustrated or excited, he would chomp down hard on his hand. He bit the thick part of the hand at the base of the thumb. At first, it was distressing for Scott and me to watch him do it because it was so frequent. It didn't take long for the area to develop a thick callous on both sides of his right hand. After some time, it didn't bother us anymore, because we knew he wasn't going to hurt himself.

A few years later he began banging his head, arm, and hand. When I say he banged them, I mean he banged them really hard. He banged them so hard that when we saw him do it, *we* winced as we imagined how it must hurt. We knew it had to be incredibly painful. He banged his head on the walls, on furniture, and on cabinets. Added to that, he didn't choose smooth surfaces. He intentionally chose the hard corners, because those provided the most stimulation for him. He banged his head on the dinner table, on his wheelchair, and on the door panels of our car. At church, he banged it on the concrete floor. He banged his head on everything! While we were visiting family one Christmas in Tennessee and Alabama, Bradley literally spent our entire one-week visit in a chair or on the couch. Whenever he was on the floor, which was hardwood flooring, he banged his head incessantly to the point where he gave himself a welt the size of a golf ball on the back of his head. After that trip, I told Scott I wouldn't travel again with Bradley for a long time, at least not until that particular behavior changed.

At its worst point, Bradley absolutely could not control himself. He was banging his head and arms nearly constantly. His forehead was full of bruises and his entire forearm was bruised from banging it on tables, walls, and his wheelchair. At this stage, Bradley's neurologist suggested a helmet for him, because he was concerned that Bradley would seriously injure himself with a concussion or further brain injury. After consulting with the neurologist, we opted not to use a helmet for two reasons. First of all, Bradley will not keep anything on his head. Second, if we found a way to keep a helmet on his head, his neurologist was afraid he would bang his head even harder in an attempt to achieve the same level of stimulation. Then he might accidentally do it with the same force while not wearing the helmet. The neurologist thought the risk of injury in that scenario was too great. Not to mention that the walls of our home would be full of holes! Instead, the neurologist suggested trying Bradley on a sedative. Scott and I weren't thrilled with the idea of him being on another medication, but we knew we had to do something. We began the sedative and in the meantime made some adjustments around the house. We began feeding Bradley on the floor in the middle of the kitchen, since he couldn't sit at the table without banging his head. The sedative helped and time passed. Eventually, the behavior began to decrease in intensity and frequency. He still bangs his head occasionally, but it is nothing like before.

Another behavioral challenge we have faced with Bradley is his tendency to throw things and, at times, be destructive around the house. Another reason we moved Bradley to eating on the floor was because he likes to throw things, and he's not discriminating about what he throws. It can be a cup, a plate, a salt shaker, or whatever he is able to reach. We had long ago switched to plastic dinnerware for him, but he has long arms and is quite fast. He can reach out and swat something off the table in a flash.

As Bradley grew older, his ability to reach higher and potentially expose himself to danger increased. He has reached to the top of our gas stove, pulled off the burners, and thrown them across the kitchen. Thankfully, when he has done this, the stove was not on and the burners were not hot. He has attempted to reach our block of sharp kitchen knives and has acquired the ability to open the doors in our house. While he can't get out of the house, our primary concern is that he could fall down our basement stairs. He has tried to pull over glass tables and plant stands, and repeatedly dug through the dirt of a large palm tree that sat in our living room. At the time we had cream-colored carpeting. What messes he made!

His most recent behavioral issues include taking off his clothes and diaper and not sleeping through the night. That poses a problem. Not only do we live in Michigan where it tends to get quite cold in the winter months, but the removal of his clothes and diaper can also create a huge mess. I won't provide details here, but, again, you can probably imagine the mess.

As far as not sleeping through the night is concerned, as you might imagine, that gets old pretty fast. When Bradley gets up in the middle of the night, he doesn't just sit quietly in his bed. He gets out of bed, takes all his clothes and diaper off, and generally destroys anything Kyle has left exposed in their bedroom. Scott and I have had to take turns sleeping on the floor of their bedroom blocking the way so that Bradley can't get out of bed.

I'm not relating all these struggles with Bradley so you'll feel sorry for us. I'm merely painting a verbal picture of how these situations have tested and strained our patience again and again. They have pushed us to our limits. We have prayed repeatedly for the various behaviors to stop. Sometimes they have diminished, sometimes they have stopped, and sometimes they have persisted. I have been exhausted mentally and physically and have been discouraged when our prayers for God's intervention weren't answered my way and in my time. I have been frustrated at having to re-diaper and re-clothe my son numerous times a day. I have been irritated at being repeatedly awakened at night with Bradley getting into things. I have been disgusted at having to clean up yet another mess.

My point is that I (we) have needed a tremendous amount of patience. And, while we wait for behaviors or situations to change, the Lord has strengthened us to keep going. Just as trust and peace come together, patience and perseverance go hand-in-hand.

One of the greatest examples of perseverance I have witnessed is the Special Olympics, in which Bradley's school participates each year. When he began attending school, Scott and I had our first opportunity to visit his school and watch the games. One year, Bradley was chosen to be the torch bearer. I think they chose him because Scott and I were both present, but, nevertheless, we were delighted. The school staff recited the Special Olympics creed:

"Please help me win, but if I cannot win, let me be brave in the attempt."

An older fellow-student pushed Bradley's wheelchair across the gym as Bradley carried the torch from one end to the other. We were moved to tears. We were so proud, but that moment wouldn't be the last time we were moved to tears. We watched kids struggle to cross the gym any way they were able. Some used walkers; some rode three-wheeled bicycles; some crawled. Some dragged themselves on their bellies across the floor, because that is all they are able to do. It was heroic.

At another Special Olympics, one of the Olympians stopped before the finish line. She had trouble finishing her race because it was hard for her to expend the effort to get that far. The entire gymnasium of people cheered her on until she was able to finish. Each time I witness one of these events, I am inspired to keep going.

No matter what I'm faced with, I know I can do it. God promises me so in Philippians 4:13. The Apostle Paul declares that with God's help, "I can do everything through him who gives me strength." He knows my limits, and He knows yours, and He will not assign to us more than we can bear.

If He has called you to do something, He will equip you to do it. Not only will He give you what you need to endure the challenge at hand, but He will allow you to triumph over it and emerge victorious in Christ!

Just like the marathon runner at the beginning of the chapter, we need patience and perseverance as we look forward to the goal. As we keep our focus on the Lord and trust Him, we persevere and take each day just as it comes. We continue putting one foot in front of the other. Just like the runner, we keep going and we don't give up. We will be encouraged by the faces of those cheering us on; fellow believers lifting us up. We can be encouraged by reading the accounts of those heroes of our faith listed in Hebrews, chapter 11. Most of all, we can look forward to hearing our Master's voice when our race is over:

> "...'Well done, good and faithful servant! You have been faithful with a few things; I will put you in charge of many things. Come and share your master's happiness!'" (Matthew 25:21 NIV).

Scriptures for Patience, Perseverance & Strength:

Romans 12:12- ...rejoicing in hope, persevering in tribulation, devoted to prayer....

Philippians 4:13- I can do all things through Him who strengthens me.

Ephesians 4:2- ...with all humility and gentleness, with patience, showing tolerance for one another in love....

1 Thessalonians 5:14- We urge you, brethren, admonish the unruly, encourage the fainthearted, help the weak, be patient with everyone.

Proverbs 19:11- A man's discretion makes him slow to anger, And it is his glory to overlook a transgression.

Galatians 5:22-23- But the fruit of the Spirit is love, joy, peace, patience, kindness, goodness, faithfulness, gentleness, self-control; against such things there is no law.

Colossians 3:12- So, as those who have been chosen of God, holy and beloved, put on a heart of compassion, kindness, humility, gentleness and patience....

Psalm 40:1- I waited patiently for the LORD; And He inclined to me and heard my cry.

Romans 5:3-5- And not only this, but we also exult in our tribulations, knowing that tribulation brings about perseverance; and perseverance, proven character; and proven character, hope; and hope does not disappoint, because the love of God has been poured out within our hearts through the Holy Spirit who was given to us.

Hebrews 12:1- Therefore, since we have so great a cloud of witnesses surrounding us, let us also lay aside every encumbrance and the sin which so easily entangles us, and let us run with endurance the race that is set before us....

James 1:2-4- Consider it all joy, my brethren, when you encounter various trials, knowing that the testing of your faith produces endurance. And let endurance have its perfect result, so that you may be perfect and complete, lacking in nothing.

2 Peter 1:5-7- Now for this very reason also, applying all diligence, in your faith supply moral excellence, and in your moral excellence, knowledge, and in your knowledge, self-control, and in your self-control, perseverance, and in your perseverance, godliness, and in your godliness, brotherly kindness, and in your brotherly kindness, love.

Hebrews 10:36- For you have need of endurance, so that when you have done the will of God, you may receive what was promised.

James 5:10-11- As an example, brethren, of suffering and patience, take the prophets who spoke in the name of the

Lord. We count those blessed who endured. You have heard of the endurance of Job and have seen the outcome of the Lord's dealings, that the Lord is full of compassion and is merciful.

Revelation 2:2-3- I know your deeds and your toil and perseverance, and that you cannot tolerate evil men, and you put to the test those who call themselves apostles, and they are not, and you found them to be false; and you have perseverance and have endured for My name's sake, and have not grown weary.

1 Corinthians 13:4a & 7- Love is patient, love is kind ... bears all things, believes all things, hopes all things, endures all things.

James 1:12- Blessed is a man who perseveres under trial; for once he has been approved, he will receive the crown of life which the Lord has promised to those who love Him.

Isaiah 41:10- Do not fear, for I am with you; Do not anxiously look about you, for I am your God. I will strengthen you, surely I will help you, Surely I will uphold you with My righteous right hand.

Isaiah 40:31- Yet those who wait for the LORD Will gain new strength; They will mount up with wings like eagles, They will run and not get tired, They will walk and not become weary.

Psalm 46:1- God is our refuge and strength, A very present help in trouble.

Romans 8:28-31- And we know that God causes all things to work together for good to those who love God, to those who are called according to His purpose. For those whom He foreknew, He also predestined to become conformed to the image of His Son, so that He would be the firstborn among many brethren; and these whom He predestined, He also called; and these whom He called, He also justified; and these whom He justified, He also glorified. What then shall we say to these things? If God is for us, who is against us?

Ephesians 1:18-21- I pray that the eyes of your heart may be enlightened, so that you will know what is the hope of His calling, what are the riches of the glory of His inheritance in the saints, and what is the surpassing greatness of His power toward us who believe. These are in accordance with the working of the strength of His might which He brought about in Christ, when He raised Him from the dead and seated Him at His right hand in the heavenly places, far above all rule and authority and power and dominion, and every name that is named, not only in this age but also in the one to come.

Galatians 6:9-10- Let us not lose heart in doing good, for in due time we will reap if we do not grow weary. So then, while we have opportunity, let us do good to all people, and especially to those who are of the household of the faith.

1 Timothy 6:12- Fight the good fight of faith; take hold of the eternal life to which you were called, and you made the good confession in the presence of many witnesses.

Chapter 6 – Smile! It's Good For You!

A joyful heart is good medicine, But a broken spirit dries up the bones (Proverbs 17:22).

Discussing a serious subject like suffering can be heavy. That being the case, let's take a little break for some comedic relief in this chapter, shall we? Though our adventures with Bradley have produced struggles, they have also produced some laughs. I'll share a couple of our humorous situations in this chapter.

Like we've always said, the only predictable thing about Bradley is that he is unpredictable. We never know what a new day will bring. Like other children, Bradley seems to go through phases.

The first story I'm going to share took place when Bradley was really into his "throwing things" stage. When he was younger, we enjoyed going out for dinner on Friday evenings as a family. We picked family-friendly establishments that tended to be noisy in case Bradley had an outburst. At times, he would throw things, whatever he could reach. He threw napkins, placemats, and utensils on the floor, and sometimes food. Ordinarily, we kept a safe radius around him so he couldn't reach anything that was on the table. But, there were those exceptions when Scott and I would either forget or were distracted. There was more than one occasion when Bradley sent a French fry sailing through the air. Scott and I held our breaths watching it fly, hoping it wouldn't land in some unsuspecting person's hair or plate. Most of the time, the renegade food landed uneventfully on the floor. However, on one occasion, we weren't so lucky.

A number of years ago, Scott and I served as supervisors for the children's department of our church. Each year we hosted an appreciation luncheon for the teachers and staff of our department at a local restaurant. One luncheon, in particular, stands out from the rest. On this occasion we chose an Italian restaurant near our church. Since we had a large party of around 15 people, we were seated at a long banquet table. All three of our children were to join us at the luncheon. As we waited to be seated, Scott and I decided it would be best to seat Bradley at the very end of the table, between the two of us. This arrangement enabled both of us to help feed him and still allow for us to participate in the conversation at the table. Our waitress brought us hot, fresh bread to eat while we waited for our main courses to arrive. We tore up a piece of bread for Bradley into bite-size pieces and spread them out on the table in front of him to feed to himself. Spreading them out reduced the number of pieces he could put into his mouth at one time (he tends to stuff his mouth full of food) and also gave Scott and me some time to talk with those around us. We chatted and were enjoying the time of fellowship.

All of a sudden, Bradley launched a piece of bread into the air. Scott and I watched it fly, almost as if in slow motion. The bread projectile sailed through the air half-way down the banquet table, and landed smack dab in the middle of the plate of one of our department's teachers. I'm telling you, it could not have been more in the center of her plate, like a bulls-eye on a target. Bradley could not have duplicated the feat if he tried a hundred more times! Of course, Scott and I apologized. Thankfully, this teacher took it all in stride and in good humor. She had been acquainted with our family for some time and was familiar with Bradley and some of his behaviors. Also, I was grateful Bradley had not chewed the bread prior to launch, which he's done before. I was a little embarrassed by the episode, but secretly, I was trying not to laugh, because it just looked so funny.

As parents of a severely disabled child in a wheelchair, we tend to draw attention wherever we go with Bradley. People, being curious, naturally notice us because we are a different type of family. Some ask questions about Bradley, and many just stare as we go by. I don't mind it as much now, but there was a time when I was more sensitive about it. Perhaps I was overly sensitive, but, nevertheless, it still bothered me. I became very irritated at the mall when people would stare at Bradley. They weren't always discreet about it either. I was amazed, at times, that even adults would crane their necks to look at us when we walked past them. I could relate to what a goldfish might feel like (if they were capable of feeling) as a person peers into his bowl to stare at him.

I was frequently stared at when I pulled into a handicapped parking space. The rear windows of our minivan were tinted, so people outside the car could not see who was in the back seat. People watched me, an able-bodied individual, get out of our van. I often received questioning glances even though I had a blue handicapped placard hanging from the rearview mirror. It was even more irritating for me, because I didn't always use these spaces. When the weather was nice or when Scott was with me, I parked in a regular parking space. However, when it was cold, or when I was by myself with all three kids, I used the handicapped parking space. People continued to stare until they saw me lift the wheelchair out of the back of the van, then they looked away. It was an encounter of this type that sets the tone for my next story.

It was a sunny summer day. Bradley was not in school, and I needed to run to the post office. It was late morning and it had already begun to be "one of those days." Kyle and Katherine had been irritating each other all morning. As a result, my nerves were on heightened alert. I piled Bradley, Kyle, and Katherine into the van, hoping the distraction of being out and away from home would help the situation. We traveled the familiar five mile route to the post office. I turned into the parking lot and quickly found a place to park – a handicapped spot on the corner of the row of parking spaces. I reached down to put my keys away and grab my purse. When I looked up, an older gentleman was staring at me from inside his car. He was driving his car very slowly in the driving lane right in front of our van, staring at me with a peculiar look on his face. I could feel my blood pressure start to rise.

Who does this guy think he is? If he had any idea what kind of situation I'm in, he'd stop staring at me!

He slowly turned the corner in front of me at a turtle's pace, continuing to stare. When he was parallel to my van, he stopped his car, still staring! By this time, I was near my boiling point. I pretended not to notice him and acted occupied with something inside my van when I could see him, out of the corner of my eye, motioning to me with his hands. I thought to myself, *I just dare you to say something to me, buddy! I can't wait to tell you why I parked here!*

My eyes betrayed everything I was feeling at that moment. I looked at him, took a deep breath, and rolled down my window. He said,

"You have something stuck in the grill of your car."

That wasn't what I expected. Perplexed, I said, "What?"

He continued, "You have a lawnmower stuck in the grill of your car."

Still not knowing what he was talking about (perhaps I misunderstood him), I thanked him and got out of the van to take a look. When I saw what was stuck in the grill, I laughed out loud – a bright green and yellow plastic, child-sized lawnmower! It was jutting precariously out from the grill at least eighteen inches!

We bought the toy mower for Kyle, because he liked to pretend he was mowing when Scott mowed the grass. He saw this particular one in the store one day and was intrigued by it. It had a handle that was hinged and folded back onto itself, like our real mower, for convenient storage. It had little beads inside it that popped when it was being used to "mow the grass." He loved it.

We kept that little mower in our garage right in front of where I parked the van. Apparently, the last time I had parked in the garage, I had pulled in a little too far and wedged the mower into the grill of the van! I can just imagine what we must have looked like cruising down the road with this thing sticking out of the front of my car! I'm sure it must have bobbed up and down with each bump of the road. It must have been a sight. No wonder that man was staring! I'm sure he wasn't the only one as we made our way down the road, completely oblivious. And to think that I almost blew up at the poor man, who was just trying to help me!

Yes, we have had our struggles with Bradley, but the Lord has intermingled laughter with difficult situations. We have learned to laugh at some of the things we used to find upsetting. Now when people stare at us, I don't become irritated. Instead, I sometimes try to initiate a conversation with them, to tell them that our situation with Bradley hasn't dealt us a death blow. I want to show them that even though we have struggles in life, with God we can still find joy and happiness. My prayer is that others will see in us the hope that is found in Christ.

The Lord is not done with Bradley, and He's not done with us either. In the chapters to follow, we will continue to explore other ways in which the Lord works for our good in all things.

Chapter 7 – Let's Get Real, People!

Bear one another's burdens, and thereby fulfill the
law of Christ (Galatians 6:2).

I'm sure most people can relate to one of the following
scenes. On the way to church, you and your husband find yourselves in a heated discussion. Instead of being resolved by the
time you pull in the church parking lot, the argument has es-
calated. You know round two will commence sometime later in
the day in the privacy and safety of your own home. You exit
your vehicle, hold your head high, and walk into church, giving
friends and acquaintances cheerful greetings as they pass.

Or – maybe the situation goes something like this. You and
your husband had guests for dinner the previous night. During
the course of the evening, your teenage son was deliberately
pushing his behavior limits by insulting his little brother in
front of your guests and their children. He knew you would not
approve of this behavior, but he did it anyway. Your dinner
guests left quite late so you put off addressing the issue until
the following day. Sunday morning comes and your rudely be-
having son doesn't want to get out of bed on time. You have to

prod him to get out of bed, adding more irritation to the events of the previous evening. He eventually gets out of bed, takes his time dressing, and is the last one in the car before leaving for church. Upon entering the vehicle, he gives his little brother a purposeful, nasty elbow to the side of the head. That was the last straw. Your blood is nearly boiling. All the way to church, you and your husband reprimand your son for his unkind, disrespectful misbehavior. Upon arrival at church, the whole family hops out of the car and walks into the sanctuary. As before, your friends are given no indication of the scene that unfolded in the car on the way to church.

Bradley's response to his world is the opposite of these scenarios. Bradley is transparent; what you see is what you get. When he is happy, you know it. When he's upset, boy, do you *really* know it! How you see him reflects exactly how he feels at that moment. He doesn't understand how to hide his feelings or even why you would want to do so. He will never be manipulative or scheming. He'll never hold a grudge against anyone. He is impartial and non-judgmental.

Maybe your situation is in some way like mine used to be. In Bradley's earlier years, when I was filled with grief, I put on my church mask. I came to church and pretended I was fine, but in reality I was a mess. When the full extent of Bradley's disability sunk in, I was absolutely heartbroken. I cried a lot. I cried at home, nearly every time I stepped into the doors of Bradley's school, and at church. I was also angry, confused, and bewildered at times, feeling as if my head was spinning. I didn't know why God was allowing this to happen in my family. I had no idea what He was trying to accomplish and I didn't like it one bit.

I didn't have a lot of support from extended family, due to geographical barriers. Our immediate and extended families are mostly scattered throughout several states. I felt isolated and alone, and as a result, I felt I had no other choice but to be strong and bear it. I did have my sister-in-law nearby, but she worked full-time and I wasn't willing to ask her for help. Although she would never view it as such, I didn't want to inconvenience her with requests for relief.

Even Scott had little idea of how I struggled through that time. Shortly after Bradley was born, Scott began experiencing serious health issues of his own and stress tended to make his symptoms worse. I wanted him to be confident in my abilities as a mother and also shield him from the added stress of my raw emotions. We rarely talked of how we felt about what we were experiencing. It was too painful and just easier to bury it. We served in various ministries in our church at the time as well. Since we have a large church, it was easy to blend in and busy ourselves with activity rather than address our needs at the time.

I thought I should have been able to handle things better than I was, and although I didn't view crying as a weakness in others, I certainly considered it so for myself. Most of all, I didn't want anyone to see me "lose it." When people asked me how I was doing at church, I quickly responded,

"Good! How are you?"

How untrue that statement was! I was afraid to share my true feelings with people. How could I tell someone that at one time I didn't *feel* love for my son? What would they think of me? How would they react if they knew there were times when I attempted to ease my frustration by banging my head on walls? Would they think I had lost my mind? I was afraid to be vulnerable, but I desperately needed help. I was drowning in sorrow, but thankfully, the Lord was keenly aware of my situation.

Even though I didn't give a voice to my grief, there was an older woman in our church who noticed my mostly-silent struggles. This dear woman of God (who has since gone home to be with our Lord) ministered to me through that time. Geri and her husband, Bill, were elders in our church and sat very near to where we were seated each week. Geri had happy, twinkling eyes and a warm, inviting smile that reminded me of my grandmother. Initially, she was drawn to us because she said Bradley, with his blond hair, reminded her of someone in their family. She watched us as we entered the service each week with Bradley. She witnessed some of his behavioral problems, and saw Scott and me leave the service on multiple occasions due to Bradley's outbursts. We alternated weeks taking him out of the service, and so were unable to attend the services together. There were times she noticed I was crying during the service. When the time came for us to stand and greet the people around us, I found she was crying for me. She hugged me tightly and told me she was praying for me. I felt the love of God through her embraces and knew that He had given her His love for us to encourage and strengthen me.

I slowly came to realize that by not sharing some of my struggles with other Christians around me, I was simply hurting myself. Galatians 6:2 tells us we should bear one another's burdens, but if the people around you don't know your pain, how can they pray for you? I have learned that the Body of Christ is beautiful in action. God does not desire for us to live in isolation, and we are not islands unto ourselves. We are all joined together in unity to share Christ with a lost and hurting world and to serve the rest of His Body.

> For even as the body is one and yet has many members, and all the members of the body, though they are many, are one body, so also is Christ. For by one

Spirit we were all baptized into one body, whether Jews or Greeks, whether slaves or free, and we were all made to drink of one Spirit. For the body is not one member, but many. If the foot says, "Because I am not a hand, I am not a part of the body," it is not for this reason any the less a part of the body. And if the ear says, "Because I am not an eye, I am not a part of the body," it is not for this reason any the less a part of the body. If the whole body were an eye, where would the hearing be? If the whole were hearing, where would the sense of smell be? But now God has placed the members, each one of them, in the body, just as He desired. If they were all one member, where would the body be? But now there are many members, but one body. And the eye cannot say to the hand, "I have no need of you"; or again the head to the feet, "I have no need of you." ... But God has so composed the body, giving more abundant honor to that member which lacked, so that there may be no division in the body, but that the members may have the same care for one another. And if one member suffers, all the members suffer with it; if one member is honored, all the members rejoice with it. Now you are Christ's body, and individually members of it (1 Corinthians 12:12-21 & 24-27).

The Lord wants us to come to Him as individuals with our deepest needs. Scripture declares that the prayers of the righteous are pleasing to God (Proverbs 15:8) and describes the prayers of the saints as incense rising continually to Him (Revelation 5:8). What a beautiful picture that is! Our prayers have a sweet aroma to our Lord! He also wants us to pray for one another, and He tells us in James 5:16 that the prayers of the righteous are powerful and effective. At times, it will be my needs that are lifted to our Lord in prayer. At other times, it will be me who carries the burdens of others heavenward. What a privilege it is to carry the needs of our brothers and sisters in Christ to the throne of our Father! Doing so fulfills the command given in Galatians to bear one another's burdens.

In hiding my emotions, I discovered I was robbing myself of the blessing of being prayed for by other saints of God. Not only that, but I may also have been missing out on the blessing of someone's assistance. There were many times I would have welcomed a helping hand. I could have used some help during some of Bradley's physical therapy appointments when Kyle was an infant, or we could have used help when Bradley was hospitalized for seizures. The list could go on and on. I didn't tell anyone, though, and certainly didn't ask for help. Again, how can someone offer to help if they aren't aware of a need? People aren't omniscient like God, and they certainly can't read your mind.

Scott is no exception; he isn't a mind-reader. Here was my high school sweetheart, my best friend on earth who loved me more than anyone else and would have done anything for me. Yet I was afraid to share my struggles and deepest feelings with him. My reactions to different situations were confusing for him at times. Sometimes I was happy; at times I was irritable and angry; and at other times I was teary for some reason he couldn't pinpoint. The poor guy! It took years for me to realize that not only was I robbing myself of being interceded for by other Christians, I also was robbing myself of a more emotionally intimate relationship with my husband.

I discovered another truth. Not only was I robbing myself of blessing, I was robbing other believers! Unknowingly, I was robbing them of an opportunity to bless another person. I don't know about you, but I love being able to bless other people. I like to help where there is a need, and I love giving gifts. Our church participates in a Prison Fellowship program called the Angel Tree. Each Christmas, prison inmates sign up their children for the program. Members of our congregation have the opportunity to sign up to purchase gifts for the children, and the gifts are delivered to the children in the name of the prisoner. Scott and I have had the opportunity to deliver some of these gifts to the families of the prisoners, and what a joy it was for us! We were a blessing to them and were, in turn, blessed by the opportunity to serve others.

There is an additional benefit when we are transparent and sincere about our trials and troubles – others will feel they aren't alone when they face storms of their own. Have you ever met someone who always seems happy, who seems like she never has a care in the world or never has a bad day? I have, and I have had a hard time establishing a real connection with that person, because I know we *all* have bad days. We all struggle with something eventually, and there is comfort in knowing that we are not alone.

Please understand that I am not advocating that we all should talk about every problem we encounter at every opportunity, nor am I recommending pity parties, a woe-is-me attitude, or the comparison of "battle" wounds. Who wants to be around someone who is always complaining about this or that? However, when we are experiencing serious issues, we should feel safe enough to share those needs with someone within the Body of Christ. I don't believe we earn any additional treasure in heaven if we stoically suffer in silence. You need someone who will pray for you, someone who will love you through your tough time. You need someone to lend a helping hand if you need it. Yes, you probably *can* do it on your own, but your situation would be so much more bearable with another believer walking alongside you lifting you up. In essence, what you really need is Jesus. How wonderful it is that He gave us people to help carry our burdens!

When my daughter Katherine was around three years old, she was terrified of butterflies. When she saw them outside, she would scream and run inside and remain there for the rest of the afternoon. Scott and I couldn't understand how anyone could be afraid of butterflies, but, nevertheless, she was. We tried to educate her about butterflies in the hope that with the increased knowledge, she would no longer be afraid of them. We told her they were harmless, beautiful creatures, and I showed her pictures of their delicate, colorful wings. We attempted to catch them so we could show her their gentleness. On one occasion, she and I spent a fun girls' day at the zoo. The zoo near our home features an exhibit on butterflies. In my motherly wisdom, I thought to myself, *There's no better way to show her that butterflies are harmless than to take her into the butterfly house! She'll see how beautiful and gentle they are and no longer mind being around them.*

When we walked into the small room adjoining the house, a zoo worker told us that the butterflies were free to flutter about their environment.

"They might be on the walking paths, so, please, watch your step. They might be on flowers and other plants within the house. They may even light on you!"

Katherine wasn't listening to the lady; she just looked around the little room as three-year-olds tend to do. We entered the house. It was filled with beautiful, fluttering, colorful butterflies! As the zoo worker had informed us, they were everywhere. One even lit on the woman's head in front of us. Katherine started crying. I tried to touch one and show her they were harmless, but she continued to cry and was getting more and more upset. I asked her if she wanted me to carry her so she wouldn't have to worry about stepping on them and so she could get a better view of the butterflies in the trees, but she didn't want that. She just wanted to get out of there as fast as possible. She was so hysterical, a worker in the house offered to let us out the emergency exit! Needless to say, my goal of decreasing her fear in butterflies failed miserably. To this day, she's not really thrilled about them.

Although the example of Katherine's fear is a bit extreme, I believe it is analogous with my situation with Bradley. My sweet little daughter was afraid, and so was I. She was afraid to be "lifted up" to see the beauty of the butterflies, and I was afraid to be vulnerable with other believers and to share my struggles with them when they could have "lifted me up" in prayer. Through Bradley's candid personality, I have learned to be more sincere in my relationships. Real ministry takes place when we remove our masks and allow ourselves to be vulnerable with other believers. I am now privileged to have a circle of believers in my life that I know will pray for me when I need it. Likewise, it is an honor and privilege for me to carry their needs to our Father. The Body of Christ is beautiful to see when it functions as intended, just like those butterflies. It is yet another way that the Lord has worked all of these things together for my good.

Chapter 8 – A Lesson in Contentment

But Godliness with contentment is great gain (1 Timothy 6:6).

Although this verse in Timothy is followed primarily by an admonition for us to avoid seeking security in material things, it has application for our discussion here as well. To have contentment is to have peace of mind, to be at ease, to be satisfied, or to be at rest.

When the realization of the severity of Bradley's disability sank into my mind, I wondered if I could ever be happy again. How could I be happy when I was reminded daily of all the things Bradley is unable to do? Would I ever be at peace, at ease, at rest, satisfied with what God was doing in our lives? Would I ever be able to say I had learned the secret of being content in any and every situation, as Paul described in Philippians 4:12?

Initially, our efforts were focused on trying to change our situation with Bradley in some way. As I mentioned previously,

I took Bradley to countless physical therapy appointments. When he was an infant and young toddler, he had trouble with balance. He often tipped over when he sat because he didn't have the strength in his trunk muscles to hold himself upright in a sitting position. The fact that he is legally blind also added to his difficulties. His eyes couldn't send visual cues to his brain about his environment. As a result, his brain couldn't send the necessary signals to his muscles to correct his posture before he fell over. During our early physical therapy appointments, the therapist tried different ways of building strength in Bradley's abdominal and back muscles. Eventually, his strength in these areas increased to the point where now no one would be able to tell that he ever had a problem sitting.

From there, our focus moved to his legs. His therapist provided strengthening exercises for him to do and also taught him how to use a walker. At times he fought her, but at other times he cooperated and walked a short distance for her using the walker. She also stretched – often painfully – his contracted hamstring muscles. As I said in chapter two, he has muscle contractures in his legs resulting from his brain injury. Every four to six months, he received twelve injections, six per leg, to paralyze the hamstring muscles. In the weeks following the injections, the therapist stretched and stretched his little legs, and he often screamed and cried because it was so painful. The goal was to stretch out the muscle and, at the same time, increase the strength of the opposing leg muscles. We were willing to go through the pain because we thought it would increase Bradley's chances to walk. It was always our hope that someday he would just get up and walk.

We also sought to change our situation through prayer. Again, in a previous chapter I mentioned that we prayed repeatedly for Bradley to be healed. These weren't isolated petitions for healing over a short period of time. We prayed for years for him to be made completely whole. Eventually, though, we came to realize that perhaps it wasn't the Lord's will to heal Bradley on this side of eternity. If that was the case, I needed help to find contentment in our situation, but I didn't need to look any further than my son.

If someone asked me to describe Bradley's personality in a few words, one of the words I would choose is *content*. Admittedly, he has his moments when he's frustrated or irritated (like we all do), but for the most part, he is content. On occasion, I sit back and just watch him. If he could communicate, what would he say? Would he ask God why he isn't able to run around and play with Kyle and Katherine outside? Would he accuse God of being unfair? His inability to communicate questions like these is outside of his control. Since he is unable to verbally communicate his feelings to us, he is unable to complain. That inability has had an impact on me. How often do I grumble about trivial things? How many times have I been upset about something that is of little value or meaning in life?

One of the ways Bradley displays his contentment is through singing. From the time he could speak, he began to sing. His singing calmed him and ministered to me. Hearing his little voice sing words filled with truth brought comfort to my heart.

> Jesus wants me for a sunbeam to shine for him each day. In every way I try to please him, at home, at school, at play. A sunbeam, a sunbeam, Jesus wants me for a sunbeam. A sunbeam, a sunbeam, I'll be a sunbeam for him.[1]

Yes, Bradley, I thought to myself, you are shining for Jesus. I hope I am, too.

> Jesus loves the little children, all the children of the world. Red and yellow, black and white, they're all precious in His sight. Jesus loves the little children of the world.[2]

Yes, Bradley, He loves you just the way you are, and He loves me, too.

> Jesus loves me this I know, for the Bible tells me so. Little ones to Him belong. They are weak, but He is strong. Yes, Jesus loves me. Yes, Jesus loves me. Yes, Jesus loves me. The Bible tells me so.[3]

Yes, Bradley, Jesus is our Good Shepherd. We are weak, but He is so very strong. He will keep us safe in the palm of His loving hands.

When he grew a bit older, he began singing some of the worship choruses and hymns we sing at our church.

> Great and mighty is the Lord, our God. Great and mighty is He.[4]

Yes, Bradley, our God is great, and He is mighty. There is none like Him and none besides Him. Nothing is too difficult for Him!

> He is Lord, He is Lord, He has risen from the dead and He is Lord.[5]

Yes, Bradley, He is Lord. Jesus Christ has risen from the dead. Our Lord conquered the grave! He is powerful! He is worthy of our trust!

My favorite song to hear Bradley sing is "Victory in Jesus" (or "Victowee," as Bradley would say). While the entire lyrics to this old hymn are meaningful, the second verse is especially touching, given Bradley's condition. Every time I heard his beautiful voice sing it, I was brought to tears.

> I heard about His healing, of His cleansing power revealing, how he made the lame to walk again and caused the blind to see; and then I cried, "Dear

Jesus, come and heal my broken spirit," and some-how Jesus came and brought to me the victory. O victory in Jesus, my Savior, forever, He sought me and He bought me with His redeeming blood; He loved me ere I knew Him, and all my love is due Him, He plunged me to victory beneath the cleansing flood.[6]

Oh, yes, my sweet Bradley, Jesus is our Redeemer, our Healer, our Victorious Savior. Thinking about these precious memories still brings me to tears.

Unknowingly, Bradley proclaimed the name of Jesus to people who may not know Him as Savior. When he was five years old, I stopped by his school to talk with his teacher and visit his classroom. His teacher at this time had heard him sing, because he sang all the time. This particular day, though, she stopped me as I was walking down the hallway.

Quite surprised, she said, "Do you know what I heard Bradley singing this morning?" I obviously hadn't heard, since I wasn't there, so she continued.

"I heard him singing a hymn!"

She went on to tell me some of the words he sang so that I could figure out the name of the song. She said,

"I haven't heard that song since I was a child at church."

He was testifying of God's goodness and grace to his teacher and other school staff in a way that only he can.

His songs are treasured memories for me. For the most part, along with his other areas of regression, this ability has disappeared as well. Within the past year or so, I've heard him sing maybe twice. I can recall with certainty that there was one instance where he briefly sang bits of "Twinkle, Twinkle Little Star." There may have been another time. Thankfully, most of the songs I have included in this chapter are recorded in his sweet voice on video.

Bradley has lost his ability, or perhaps his desire, to sing for the most part, but that's okay. I am at a different stage of our journey now. I am no longer trying to change our situation. I still do things I believe are going to help Bradley develop to his fullest potential, but my prayers now aren't focused on God removing this situation from us. Don't get me wrong. If God offered complete healing for Bradley tomorrow, I wouldn't refuse it! In fact, I'd be ecstatic! But, as long as it seems to be His will for that not to happen right now, I am content. I have learned to accept our situation and learn from it. Instead of praying for the Lord to take us *out* of this situation, I am now praying that He would use us *in* and *through* it. I pray for Him to help me be the best mother I can be for Bradley. I pray for Him to show me what He wants me to learn from Bradley. I pray for opportunities to be a witness of God's goodness, even in a situation like ours, to those who don't know Him. I pray for other parents of children like Bradley who don't have the hope I have in Christ.

Hold on a minute, though. I'm getting ahead of myself here. We'll get into this more in the next chapter.

My emphasis here is that we have reached the point of acceptance in our journey with Bradley. Can we be at peace if he can never communicate with us? Can we be at ease with our circumstance if Bradley never walks? Can we be at rest with the fact that he will probably always wear diapers? Can we be satisfied with where God has placed us? Can we be happy? The answer is an emphatic, "Absolutely!" Our joy is not found in the inherent "goodness" or "badness" of our circumstances. We can have joy in our lives regardless of our situation!

> ...though you have not seen Him, you love Him, and though you do not see Him now, but believe in Him, you greatly rejoice with joy inexpressible and full of glory, obtaining as the outcome of your faith the salvation of your souls (1 Peter 1:8-9).

We have joy because Jesus Christ purchased our salvation! We can rest in the assurance that no matter what is swirling about us, He is in control and He is still on His throne. Not only that, we look forward to the ultimate fulfillment of Scripture when we get to spend eternity with Him! I'm getting ahead of myself here, too. More will follow on this topic as well, and I can't wait to tell you about it!

Scriptures on Contentment, Rest, and Joy:

Philippians 4:11-13- Not that I speak from want, for I have learned to be content in whatever circumstances I am. I know how to get along with humble means, and I also know how to live in prosperity; in any and every circumstance I have learned the secret of being filled and going hungry, both of having abundance and suffering need. I can do all things through Him who strengthens me.

Hebrews 13:5-6- Make sure that your character is free from the love of money, being content with what you have; for He Himself has said, "I WILL NEVER DESERT YOU, NOR WILL I EVER FORSAKE YOU," so that we confidently say, "THE LORD IS MY HELPER, I WILL NOT BE AFRAID. WHAT WILL MAN DO TO ME?" (The phrase "being content with what you have" can be applied to our circumstances as well as our view of the material world. We can be content with whatever situation God has placed us in.)

Psalm 91:1-2- He who dwells in the shelter of the Most High Will abide in the shadow of the Almighty. I will say to the LORD, "My refuge and my fortress, My God, in whom I trust!" (When we are sheltered by our God, we can find rest in the comfort of His presence.)

Jeremiah 6:16- Thus says the LORD, "Stand by the ways and see and ask for the ancient paths, Where the good way is, and walk in it; And you will find rest for your souls...."

Matthew 11:28-30- Come to Me, all who are weary and heavy-laden, and I will give you rest. Take My yoke upon you and learn from Me, for I am gentle and humble in heart, and YOU WILL FIND REST FOR YOUR SOULS. For My yoke is easy and My burden is light. (Jesus speaking)

Psalm 4:7- You have put gladness in my heart, More than when their grain and new wine abound.

Psalm 21:6- For You make him most blessed forever; You make him joyful with gladness in Your presence.

Psalm 51:12- Restore to me the joy of Your salvation And sustain me with a willing spirit.

Habakkuk 3:18- ...Yet I will exult in the LORD, I will rejoice in the God of my salvation.

John 15:11- These things I have spoken to you so that My joy may be in you, and that your joy may be made full. (Jesus speaking)

1 Thessalonians 5:16-18- Rejoice always; pray without ceasing; in everything give thanks; for this is God's will for you in Christ Jesus.

Psalm 118:24- This is the day which the LORD has made; Let us rejoice and be glad in it.

Philippians 4:4- Rejoice in the Lord always; again I will say, rejoice!

Isaiah 61:10- I will rejoice greatly in the LORD, My soul will exult in my God; For He has clothed me with garments of salvation, He has wrapped me with a robe of righteousness....

Chapter 9 – Made For Ministry

Blessed be the God and Father of our Lord Jesus Christ, the Father of mercies and God of all comfort, who comforts us in all our affliction so that we will be able to comfort those who are in any affliction with the comfort with which we ourselves are comforted by God. For just as the sufferings of Christ are ours in abundance, so also our comfort is abundant through Christ. But if we are afflicted, it is for your comfort and salvation; or if we are comforted, it is for your comfort, which is effective in the patient enduring of the same sufferings which we also suffer; and our hope for you is firmly grounded, knowing that as you are sharers of our sufferings, so also you are sharers of our comfort (2 Corinthians 1:3-7).

You want me to do **what**, Lord?!

A few years ago I was asked to speak at a women's ministry gathering at our church. My church has a fairly large congregation, and our women's ministry hosts a couple of big events annually. This occasion, the Women's Breakfast, is the largest of the events and usually packs our church's chapel with about four hundred women! These women come hungry in more ways than one. They are nourished with a delicious meal, of course, but they also look forward to hearing a testimony of how the Lord has helped a woman of our congregation. I had attended several of these breakfasts in the past and was always blessed by the message delivered by each speaker.

I was approached several months prior to the event by our Director of Women's Ministries. When she asked me if I would be willing to speak at the breakfast, I wasn't at all surprised. Scared? Yes! Surprised? No. God had been preparing me for months, even years, for this opportunity, though I had not shared His leading with anyone. In fact, the following quote is recorded in my journal over a year before the breakfast.

"I've been reflecting a lot lately about the experiences of my life and where God has brought me to this point.... I'm feeling as though the Lord wants me to share it publicly at some point."

I agreed to the request to speak and began preparation of my presentation, which was scheduled to last about forty-five minutes. I was scared, but I was also excited. I had never spoken in front of so many people for so long a time. I was eager to share what God had done for me, individually, in accepting Him as Savior (my personal testimony), and what He had taught me (and continues to teach me) through our experiences with Bradley (my TEST-imony). I looked forward to sharing with the women in attendance the faithfulness, grace, and mercy of our Lord, and I wanted them to be encouraged and comforted by what the Lord had done in our situation. I realized that had it not been for our current circumstance, I likely would not have had the privilege of speaking to those four hundred women.

All too often, we neglect our relationship with the Lord when life is sailing along smoothly. We may become complacent, too comfortable, and perhaps even stagnant in our spiritual growth. We may not devote as much time to prayer as we should, or we might neglect reading and meditating on His life-changing, powerful Word. God wants to use our lives as a witness of His love and mercy to those who don't know Him and as an encouragement to those who do know Him. He wants to use us, but first He has to grab our attention.

Consider the account of Saul in Acts 9. Saul was a devout Jew, a student of the Law, who zealously pursued and subsequently persecuted followers of a new movement referred to as "the Way." Traveling to Damascus with the purpose of weeding out more followers of the Way in the synagogues, Saul had an encounter with Jesus Christ. He was halted in his tracks by a blinding light and the voice of Jesus speaking,

"Saul, Saul, why do you persecute me?"

"Who are you, Lord?" Saul asked.

The Lord revealed Himself, continuing, "I am Jesus, whom you are persecuting. Now get up and go into the city, and you will be told what you must do."

Saul was led into Damascus by the men who were traveling with him where, after three days, he was met and prayed for by a disciple named Ananias. Through Ananias, God healed Saul's blindness and filled him with the Holy Spirit. From this point forward, Saul began to spread the good news of the Gospel of Jesus Christ everywhere he went. After his conversion, he ardently preached and taught of the grace and mercy of God, through His Son, Jesus Christ, with as much zeal (or more) as when he persecuted the early believers.

Although most of us won't have an encounter like that of Saul, the Lord's means of halting us in our tracks are quite effective. He can use our experiences in suffering to drive us to Him and, eventually, help us to die to ourselves. During trying times, we learn to deny ourselves and develop more selflessness. In essence, we are placed in situations to build godly character within us. We will face circumstances that challenge us in every aspect, and in the process we will begin to think less of ourselves and fulfilling our selfish desires. At the same time, godly characteristics are being built and refined.

> ..."If anyone wishes to come after Me, he must deny himself, and take up his cross daily and follow Me. For whoever wishes to save his life will

lose it, but whoever loses his life for My sake, he is the one who will save it" (Luke 9:23-24; Jesus speaking).

There have been times in caring for Bradley when I have missed out on fun activities, social functions, or weekends away because of my obligations at home. I would be less than honest if I said those times didn't bother me. *Of course*, they bothered me! However, if we can train ourselves to keep a proper perspective, we can begin to view the situations in our lives as a ministry. Consider the verse from Luke above. What does it mean to take up our cross?

Try to imagine what occurred in those days of the Roman Empire when a criminal carried his own cross. The individual knew he was carrying, on his own back, the very implement to be used in his death. Thankfully, we don't face physical death by crucifixion in modern times (with maybe a few rare exceptions), but we do have figurative crosses to carry. We carry those situations which serve to crucify parts of us that the Lord is seeking to transform or even remove. As we mature in our relationship with God, we should see less and less of our old, selfish ways. In their place, we should begin to see more traits that reflect Christ living in us through the power of the Holy Spirit. As Paul declares in Galatians 2:20,

I have been crucified with Christ; and it is no longer I who live, but Christ lives in me; and the life which I now live in the flesh I live by faith in the Son of God, who loved me and gave Himself up for me.

Our lives become a ministry when we focus on Jesus in the midst of our circumstances. I love how Jesus describes our service to Him in Matthew 25:34-40.

"Then the King will say to those on His right, 'Come, you who are blessed of My Father, inherit the kingdom prepared for you from the foundation of the world. For I was hungry, and you gave Me something to eat; I was thirsty, and you gave Me something to drink; I was a stranger, and you invited Me in; naked, and you clothed Me; I was sick, and you visited Me; I was in prison, and you came to Me.' Then the righteous will answer Him, 'Lord, when did we see You hungry, and feed You, or thirsty, and give You something to drink? And when did we see You a stranger, and invite You in, or naked, and clothe You? When did we see You sick, or in prison, and come to You?' The King will answer and say to them, 'Truly I say to you, to the extent that you did it to one of these brothers of Mine, even the least of them, you did it to Me.'"

So I ask myself, Would I do all the things for Jesus that I do for Bradley? Absolutely! Would I continue to do those things for our Lord in the presence of discomfort and fatigue? Would I gladly give up things I would normally like to do to care for Him? The answer is an emphatic, unequivocal yes! When I think of my efforts in this way, I find strength to continue on, because when I serve others I know I am serving my Lord. Paul reinforces this idea in Colossians 3:23-24.

> Whatever you do, do your work heartily, as for the Lord rather than for men, knowing that from the Lord you will receive the reward of the inheritance. It is the Lord Christ whom you serve.

God has a divine assignment for each one of us. John 17 records Jesus praying. First, he prayed for Himself. Then He prayed for His disciples. He says:

> "I do not ask You to take them out of the world, but to keep them from the evil one.... As You sent Me into the world, I also have sent them into the world.... I do not ask on behalf of these alone, but for those also who believe in Me through their word; that they may all be one; even as You, Father, are in Me and I in You, that they also may be in Us, so that the world may believe that You sent Me (John 17:15, 18 & 20-21).

Do you find it interesting that Jesus did not ask that we be protected from heartache? Did you notice that He didn't ask that we be sheltered from hardship? If the Lord removed us from our difficult situations, we couldn't witness to others through it. We have not only an opportunity, but also a *responsibility*, to testify to the sustaining grace and mercy of God. It is our job to declare that with Christ we can be victorious in any situation!

Several years ago, our pastor delivered a series of sermons which aimed to help members of our church discover their God-given abilities. The discovery of these gifts could be used to point an individual to an area of ministry within the church. Our pastor made a statement at the time that resonated with me. She said,

"The experiences of your life can shape you for service."

It made sense when I thought about it, but I had never thought of ministry that way before. I learned that I will be most effective in ministry where I can most relate with the people being ministered to. For example, if you have had diffi-culties with substance abuse and God has delivered you from those addictions, you will certainly have a unique perspective to share with others experiencing similar problems. Likewise, if you've experienced the heartache of divorce, you will have em-pathy with others going through the same struggle and be able to help them. I'm not saying you can't minister effectively in an area where you haven't experienced similar situations person-ally, but often God gives us a heart for people who share bur-dens similar to what we are carrying or have carried in the past. Furthermore, He can give us the knowledge and wisdom to help them in their struggle.

Another older woman of our church was a good example of this principle in action (she has since gone home to be with our Lord). This dear lady, Judy, called me a few weeks after Bradley was born to ask me how he was doing and to pray with me over the phone. She had heard requests for prayer for us at church when Bradley was still in the hospital. I had never met her before and didn't know anything about her. When she first heard those prayer requests for Bradley, something stirred within her. God had given her a special love for my son and, of course, I was touched that she cared for him. Her love and kindness also reminded me that the Lord was mindful of us and what we were going through.

Once we settled into a routine after bringing Bradley home from the hospital, we made arrangements to meet with Judy after church so she could meet him. She was quiet and soft-spoken but was clearly pleased that she had the opportunity to meet us. Not long after this initial contact, she became primarily homebound because of her own health issues, but she called me regularly to get an update on how he was doing. She would always ask,

"How's my baby doing?"

She continued to call him her baby even when Bradley grew older. This gentle woman personified the faithfulness of God. She continued to call me regularly for many years to check on

Bradley and always to pray with me. I eventually found out through our conversations that her son had special needs as well. He wasn't as significantly impaired as Bradley, but the Lord had softened her heart to people in circumstances such as ours. He turned the sorrow of her experience into an effective ministry. Although she often couldn't leave her own home, she could minister by phone to someone in need.

God wants to use us to reach others through our circumstances. We need to allow ourselves to be willing vessels in His hands. Often, our area of ministry will be similar to what we have experienced. He can use us to comfort others in similar situations "with the comfort we ourselves have received from God" (2 Corinthians 1:4). Others can be encouraged by our example when they see us continue to strive and persevere in the midst of difficulty.

As I said in the previous chapter, my focus has changed. I am sure that I have grown more spiritually over the last fourteen years with Bradley than I ever might have without our trials. Our experiences in adversity hasten our spiritual development. Instead of praying for the Lord to take us *out* of this situation, I am now praying that He will use us *in* and *through* it. I pray for Him to show me what He wants me to learn from Bradley, and that includes a responsibility to share what I've learned with others. I pray for opportunities to be a witness of

God's goodness, even in a situation like ours, to those who don't know Him. I pray that Christ will be so reflected through my life that, as Jesus prayed in John 17, the world (at least in my sphere of influence) would believe that He was sent by the Father and that He is who He says He is in His Word. He *is* faithful! He *is* merciful! He *is* love! He *is* gracious! He *is* with us and helps us in our struggles to produce the person He desires for us to be!

Like my older sister in Christ who ministered to me, I have become more sensitive to others in situations similar to my own. I pray for other parents of children like Bradley who don't have the hope that I have in Christ. I truly cannot imagine being in my shoes without Him! I pray that this book will be a blessing to these precious people. I pray that they will be led to seek our precious Savior in the midst of their situation. I pray that they will call out to Him, the One who is very near, and experience the perfect peace that only He gives. I want them to have the assurance that I have. Yes, our God *can and will* work *all things* together for good for those who love Him! But that's not all. We have some awesome promises to look forward to in the future!

Scriptures Relating to Our Opportunities for Ministry:

Proverbs 3:27- Do not withhold good from those to whom it is due, When it is in your power to do it.

Galatians 6:9-10- Let us not lose heart in doing good, for in due time we will reap if we do not grow weary. So then, while we have opportunity, let us do good to all people, and especially to those who are of the household of the faith.

Ephesians 2:10- For we are His workmanship, created in Christ Jesus for good works, which God prepared before-hand so that we would walk in them.

Ephesians 5:1-2- Therefore be imitators of God, as beloved children; and walk in love, just as Christ also loved you and gave Himself up for us, an offering and a sacrifice to God as a fragrant aroma.

Philippians 2:3-4- Do nothing from selfishness or empty conceit, but with humility of mind regard one another as more important than yourselves; do not merely look out for your own personal interests, but also for the interests of others.

Chapter 10 – Hope Redirected

> Therefore we do not lose heart, but though our outer man is decaying, yet our inner man is being renewed day by day. For momentary, light affliction is producing for us an eternal weight of glory far beyond all comparison, while we look not at the things which are seen, but at the things which are not seen; for the things which are seen are temporal, but the things which are not seen are eternal (2 Corinthians 4:16-18).

As we mature in our faith, our circumstances should be viewed in light of their eternal value and not our present discomfort. God certainly views our troubles that way. Think of the instances in the Bible where God's people went through trials. Sometimes the reason for their troubles was revealed, while other times it was withheld. The Lord apparently isn't as concerned with our comfort as He is with our growth and maturity. He focuses on things which will have an eternal, lasting value. He is willing to allow us to be uncomfortable, to squirm, to be in pain, to be heartbroken, because He sees the end result.

One of my favorite Biblical characters is Joseph. Joseph was familiar with hardship. He was reviled by his brothers who sold him into slavery in Egypt. He was falsely accused of seducing Potiphar's wife and put into prison for a number of years.

Being taken to Egypt, I imagine Joseph was filled with many questions. *Why me, God? Why do my brothers hate me so much? I can't help the fact that my father favors me over them, nor can I help that You gave me those dreams. It's not my fault. Will I ever see my father and my homeland again?*

In Egypt, he encountered Potiphar's wife.

Lord, you know I'm innocent! Please step in and do something! Don't let me be put into a prison for something I didn't do! This isn't fair!

In prison, Joseph may have felt forgotten by God. He was certainly forgotten by his fellow prisoners. After interpreting the dreams of Pharaoh's cupbearer and baker, Joseph was hopeful the cupbearer would remember him when he was restored to his former position under Pharaoh. The cupbearer forgot about Joseph for two long years, until Pharaoh had a troubling dream which his magicians and wise men were unable to interpret. Only then did the cupbearer remember Joseph and his ability to interpret dreams. Being brought before Pharaoh, Joseph was able to interpret Pharaoh's dream. As a result of this, Pharaoh placed Joseph in charge of his own household and all of Egypt, second only to Pharaoh himself. In that position, Joseph was able to prepare for an unprecedented famine throughout the entire land. The lives of the people of Egypt and surrounding regions were spared because Joseph was placed in charge. More importantly, God preserved His chosen people, the Israelites, through Joseph.

Eventually, Joseph recognized the purpose behind his suffering. After revealing his identity to his brothers, who were undoubtedly fearful of retribution by their now very powerful brother, Joseph told them,

> "Now do not be grieved or angry with yourselves, because you sold me here, for God sent me before you to preserve life. For the famine has been in the land these two years, and there are still five years in which there will be neither plowing nor harvesting. God sent me before you to preserve for you a remnant in the earth, and to keep you alive by a great deliverance. Now, therefore, it was not you who sent me here, but God; and He has made me a father to Pharaoh and lord of all his household and ruler over all the land of Egypt" (Genesis 45:5-8).

I shared previously that when Bradley was younger, I questioned why God would allow him (and us) to experience such difficulty. Why didn't He allow my son to be born completely healthy like so many others? Why did severe disability strike him and not me? In addition to his other difficulties, why did he have to be legally blind, too?

Joseph's story encourages me. He suffered in many ways for years, but the purpose for his suffering was eventually revealed to him. I find comfort in the fact that Joseph discovered the reason behind the hardships he experienced. It may not be until I see my Savior face to face, but I am hopeful that one day we will understand the answers to those "why" questions and be able to look back and see the beautiful tapestry God has woven from our circumstances.

Let us also consider the man born blind in the New Testament (John 9). Certainly he and his parents were acquainted with suffering. I'm sure his parents experienced grief as they mourned the loss of their dreams for their son. Parents always have hopes and expectations for the life of a child. I'm sure his parents mourned his inability to play as other children did when he was young. I'm sure they mourned his inability to learn a trade and support himself and a family. It may have been humiliating for them to see their son a beggar. I'm sure the son wondered why he had been born blind. He surely longed for the abilities and skills he lacked.

The blind man and his parents were the recipients of scorn. It was a commonly held belief at the time that circumstances like this were a result of sin. People around them, including the disciples, asked the question,

> ..."Rabbi, who sinned, this man or his parents, that
> he would be born blind?" Jesus answered, "It was
> neither that this man sinned, nor his parents; but
> it was so that the works of God might be displayed
> in him" (John 9:2-3).

It isn't clear whether the man's parents heard Jesus' reply. If they did, I imagine a tremendous burden of guilt and relief would have been lifted from them. The nagging question, "Did *we* do something to cause this to happen to our son?" would have been instantly silenced as they realized God had a purpose for their suffering. Jesus went on to miraculously heal the man and display His mighty power to the blind man, his parents, the disciples, others who knew the man, and also the Pharisees. The healed man and his parents could then view their years of suffering from an entirely different perspective. Perhaps they could now see how their situation was used to testify of God's power. Even more amazing, their story also testifies to us today through His Word nearly two thousand years later!

Undoubtedly, the greatest example of suffering in the history of the world is Jesus Himself. The Son of God humbled Himself, took on human flesh, and came to redeem mankind. In a human body, Jesus put a face on God, and made God approachable for us. He perfectly reflected the nature of the Father for all to see. He exhibited unfathomable wisdom that confounded the Pharisees and Sadducees. He demonstrated

His power by performing miracles. He fed thousands of people from a quantity of food that would have only been enough for a few individuals. He calmed a storm on the Sea of Galilee. He walked on water. He healed the blind, the mute, the demon-possessed, and the sick that were brought to him. He cleansed lepers. He had the ability to raise the dead! Everywhere He went, He taught His disciples and others about God's kingdom and His purposes.

In all of these things, Jesus showed those around Him, and us, God's tremendous love and concern for humanity. He is touched by our circumstances, although we may not always sense it. He was moved to tears when He saw His friend Mary – and others with her – mourning the death of her dear brother, Lazarus. He wept over Jerusalem and its inhabitants. He came to save His own people, yet they didn't recognize Him. The Jewish people didn't realize their long-awaited, promised Messiah and Savior was standing in their midst.

Jesus had done nothing to deserve the treatment He eventually received. Certainly, there has been no greater injustice in the history of humanity. The perfect, sinless, Son of God was falsely accused of blasphemy. He was betrayed by one of His own disciples, deserted by His closest friends, mocked and ridiculed, spat upon, beaten, and ultimately crucified. I can only imagine Mary's horror as she watched her beloved Son on the cross. She had witnessed His miracles, too. Why was Jesus allowing these things to happen? She knew He had the power to prevent them. I'm sure she was utterly heartbroken and stricken with grief to see her precious Son's body covered in blood.

Mary could not foresee how good was to come of this, but the Father could. Our Heavenly Father was willing to allow His perfect Son to unjustly suffer and die because of the resulting good. The Father knew Jesus would be the firstborn of many brothers (Romans 8:29). As a result of His perfect work on the cross and His resurrection a few days later, there are untold numbers of people who have gained eternal life!

Even though we will continue to suffer on this earth in one way or another, we have hope in Christ and what He has done for us. That is exciting! With our focus shifted away from our temporal circumstances and on to eternity, we have much to look forward to! The Bible is full of promises of hope for our future. There will come a time when all sickness and suffering will end. There will be no more death, nor anymore tears.

> A highway will be there, a roadway, And it will be called the Highway of Holiness. The unclean will not travel on it, But it will be for him who walks that way, And fools will not wander on it. No lion will be there, Nor will any vicious beast go up on it; These will not be found there. But the redeemed will walk there, And the ransomed of the LORD will return And come with joyful shouting to Zion,

With everlasting joy upon their heads. They will find gladness and joy, And sorrow and sighing will flee away (Isaiah 35:8-10).

This hope is further described in Revelation 7:17:

For the Lamb in the center of the throne will be their shepherd, and will guide them to springs of the water of life; and God will wipe every tear from their eyes.

Scott and I have both received small glimpses of our future hope for Bradley. We've both experienced dreams on multiple occasions in which Bradley was walking and talking with us. Those dreams were wonderful. I recall awakening feeling the joy of having seen him walking, yet at the same time being saddened, because it wasn't our reality (at least not right now).

The Lord has also given other instances when this glimpse of hope for Bradley's future was bolstered. When Bradley was around six or seven years old, we took all three of our children to an indoor water park for a fun-filled evening together. Bradley loves the water, so we knew he would have a wonderful time. The water park contained different areas to accommodate the varied ability levels of swimmers. There was a zero-entry pool for toddlers with water cannons and waterfalls, a water slide, and also a lazy river with deeper water. We purchased a flotation device that fastened around Bradley's neck to help keep his head and face out of the water. There were lifeguards on duty, but Katherine was still quite small, so I kept a close eye on her in the toddler area. Scott, Bradley, and Kyle played nearby in deeper water. Scott's voice caught my attention. He said excitedly,

"Honey! Bradley's walking!"

I turned and saw one of the most beautiful sights I've ever seen. Bradley was walking unassisted through the deeper water, with a look of concentration and satisfaction on his face. The water provided enough buoyancy to help his weak legs hold his body up. I instantly began to cry. I didn't want to take my eyes off of him so I could soak in that visual picture and remember what he looked like walking.

1 Corinthians 15:42-44 declares:

> So also is the resurrection of the dead. It is sown a perishable body, it is raised an imperishable body; it is sown in dishonor, it is raised in glory; it is sown in weakness, it is raised in power; it is sown a natural body, it is raised a spiritual body. If there is a natural body, there is also a spiritual body.

We know we will see Bradley walking again one day, and on that day it won't be in a swimming pool! One day, he will not be limited by the inabilities of his earthly body. In heaven, he will walk, run, and jump in his newly restored heavenly body. Perhaps he won't stop running!

Bradley also enjoys playing catch. He especially enjoyed it when he was younger. Scott and I are both fairly athletic, so we enjoy being outside in the summer months with the kids playing various games. During the times we were outdoors, we brought Bradley out to join us in his wheelchair. We took turns playing catch with him so he would stay content being out with us. We threw a basketball, or something similar, to him while he was sitting in his wheelchair so that the ball landed in his lap. He would hold it for sometimes ten to twenty seconds, and then he would quickly throw it and say,

"Shoot!"

Sometimes his shot went straight forward; sometimes it went sideways; and at times it even flipped backward over his head! In heaven, I won't be at all surprised that not only will he run and jump, but he will also be able to dunk a basketball! That will be a sight to see!

In heaven, there will be no more seizures, no more medications, no difficulty eating, no muscle contractures, and no more painful injections in his legs. Bradley's vision will be perfectly clear. We will again hear his beautiful voice singing the praises of His Redeemer. Then he will sing with strength in his voice. He'll sing loudly and clearly with a choir of other believers and angels.

I think what we will look forward to most of all is just talking to our precious boy. Most of his thoughts are hidden from us, because he lacks the ability to express himself with words. We know the things that he likes and dislikes in a basic way, because he either accepts or rejects them. In heaven, we will be able to communicate with him in a way we never have before. We will have in-depth conversations with him. He will have the ability to tell us everything he has ever wanted to tell us but couldn't. We will have an eternity together enjoying all that our Savior has prepared for us.

Until then, our focus remains on the current tasks God has assigned for us. The troubles we experience now are only temporary. Our trials will be painful, but they will have an end. *They will pass.* There is purpose behind our suffering. The Lord may or may not choose to reveal that purpose during our lifetime here on earth, but we can trust Him now and for our future. We can enthusiastically continue on the journey He has marked out for us. I don't want to barely make it across the finish line of the race marked out for me. I don't want to crawl or drag myself across the line. I want to run across it filled with faith, vigor and confidence – not confidence in myself, but confidence in the promises of our God.

God could have kept Joseph from his hardships. He could have kept the man from being born blind. He could have intervened so His beloved Son wouldn't suffer. But He didn't. He saw the end result. He knew the benefits that would flow from each situation. He knows the blessings that have been and will be wrought in my life and in my family through our experiences with Bradley, and He knows the same about your situation.

We are truly the recipients of a treasure, but not a treasure that the world understands. We hold a treasure when we hold God's Word and His promises for us. We are the privileged beneficiaries of centuries of supernatural preservation of His Word to mankind. Because of this, we can look back from our place in history and see account after account of how God has purposefully and wonderfully woven good from bad situations. What a blessing we have in His Word! In it, He has promised to work *in all things* for our good. We can be encouraged that whatever we face, He is faithful and is right there loving, helping, strengthening, guiding, encouraging, shaping, and equipping us. Thank You, Lord!

Additional Scriptures Related to Our Eternal Focus:

Psalm 30:11-12- You have turned for me my mourning into dancing; You have loosed my sackcloth and girded me with gladness, That my soul may sing praise to You and not be silent. O LORD my God, I will give thanks to You forever.

Psalm 126:5- Those who sow in tears shall reap with joyful shouting.

Jeremiah 31:13- ...For I will turn their mourning into joy And will comfort them and give them joy for their sorrow.

Luke 6:21- ...Blessed are you who weep now, for you shall laugh.

Philippians 3:14 & 20-21- I press on toward the goal for the prize of the upward call of God in Christ Jesus... For our citizenship is in heaven, from which also we eagerly wait for a Savior, the Lord Jesus Christ; who will transform the body of our humble state into conformity with the body of His glory, by the exertion of the power that He has even to subject all things to Himself.

Colossians 3:1-4- Therefore if you have been raised up with Christ, keep seeking the things above, where Christ is, seated at the right hand of God. Set your mind on the things above, not on the things that are on earth. For you have died and your life is hidden with Christ in God. When Christ, who is our life, is revealed, then you also will be revealed with Him in glory.

Hebrews 11:13-16- All these died in faith, without receiving the promises, but having seen them and having welcomed them from a distance, and having confessed that they were strangers and exiles on the earth. For those who say such things make it clear that they are seeking a country of their own. And indeed if they had been thinking of that country from which they went out, they would have had opportunity to return. But as it is, they desire a better country, that is, a heavenly one. Therefore God is not ashamed to be called their God; for He has prepared a city for them.

Conclusion

But He knows the way I take; When He has tried
me, I shall come forth as gold. My foot has held
fast to His path; I have kept His way and not
turned aside. I have not departed from the command of His lips; I have treasured the words of His
mouth more than my necessary food (Job 23:10-12).

Job was a man of great faith and experienced what must
have been the most difficult season of his life. His worldly
wealth had been stripped away; all of his children had died
when a roof collapsed on them; he had been stricken with
painful sores all over his body; and his wife was less than understanding. Adding to Job's misery, friends came to counsel
and "comfort" him, accusing Job of hidden sin and wrongdo-
ing. It was during the discourse with his friends that Job made
the above statement. His words reflect a quiet trust, resolute-
ness, and determination to remain committed to God. Job realized that he was being tested and had the assurance that God
was aware of his situation. In the midst of his suffering and re-
criminations of his friends, he was able to see some benefit to
his suffering. ("I will come forth as gold," verse 10.) I wonder

what the fruit of Job's suffering looked like. We are told that the latter part of Job's life was blessed even more than the first part, but how did his suffering change him on the inside? We know from the beginning of the book that he was blameless and upright before his trial, but how were those traits refined? Did he have a more eternal perspective after seeing everything he possessed taken away? Was he more compassionate toward others who were suffering? Was he emboldened to declare the goodness of God to those who didn't know Him?

The Bible doesn't provide us with the answers to those questions, but we do know that the character of God is immutable. In other words, He doesn't change. When He promised to work all things together for the good of His people in the New Testament, we know that He also did the same for His people living in Old Testament times.

As was the case with Job, God has chosen not to reveal to Scott and me why Bradley was born the way he was. God knows our frame and sees our lives in their entirety, while we see only our current snapshot in time and the events that have already occurred. He knows our inclinations and weaknesses. Maybe God allowed our situation with Bradley so that we wouldn't become prideful. Paul's "thorn in the flesh" was given for this reason (2 Corinthians 12:7). Maybe we would have become too comfortable and reached a point where we thought we didn't need God. Maybe God spared not only Scott and me, but also Kyle and Katherine, and maybe even our grandchildren, from straying from Him. We don't really know. However, our experiences with Bradley have given us a hunger for heaven and eternity, a hunger which we have endeavored to pass on to our children. We don't know how Bradley's life is affecting the lives of others, nor do we know how it will affect Kyle and Katherine as they grow to adulthood. Nevertheless, I would rather have Bradley like he is with our family following Christ than to have Bradley completely whole without Christ. Without Christ, nothing else matters!

Whatever God's reasons for allowing His people to suffer, His motivation is always love. He loves us too much to leave us where we are when we first come to salvation. It is because of His love for us that He gives us opportunities to grow spiritually, which is His desire for us. Our pain is beneficial because our insufficiencies drive us to our Heavenly Father. When we are scared and insecure, we come to the end of ourselves and are reminded how much we need God.

God's transforming work in us begins when we run to Him, admitting our weakness in humility. I came across an analogy recently that reminded me of the value of suffering. Although it was written in 1948 and the numbers are outdated, the principles behind it still apply today:

It is said that a bar of steel worth $5 when made into ordinary horseshoes will be worth only $10. If this same $5 bar is made into needles, the value rises to $350, but if it is made into delicate springs for expensive watches, it will be worth $250,000. This original bar of steel is made more valuable by being cut to its proper size, passed through the heat again and again, hammered and manipulated, beaten and pounded, finished and polished, until it is finally ready for its delicate task.[7]

God teaches us through suffering those things we can't learn any other way. He refines us, disciplines us, sustains us, and keeps us close to Him. In doing so, He builds our character, increases our faith, matures us, and gives us hope for a future where we will rule and reign with Him. As only He is able to do, He weaves all of these together to make us more effective witnesses for Christ in a lost and hurting world.

Throughout this book, I have shared lessons we have learned through our experiences with our oldest son, Bradley. We haven't learned these principles perfectly, but when we face difficult times, we are quickly reminded of all the times the Lord has worked for good through our circumstances and met all our needs. James 1:2-4 says,

Consider it all joy, my brethren, when you encounter various trials, knowing that the testing of your faith produces endurance. And let endurance have its perfect result, so that you may be perfect and complete, lacking in nothing.

This statement puts to rest any argument that the life of a Christian will be, or even should be, carefree and smooth-sailing. James tells us that not only will we face trials, but trials of many kinds. From there, though, he immediately shifts his focus to the resulting blessing of those trials.

I'll admit that I'm not initially joyful when difficult times come my way, but when some time has passed and I have had time to reflect on these experiences, I am able to see some benefit in each situation.

Although we never would have chosen to walk the path we are walking with Bradley, the Lord has blessed us in many ways and taught us many things. We will certainly face times of pain and heartache, but the Lord is there to comfort us and give us hope through His many promises. When we are filled with fear and uncertainty, the Holy Spirit is there building our trust in Him and filling us with His peace. When it seems like we are laboring endlessly, the Lord is there developing patience within us and strengthening us to continue persevering until our assignment is complete. He is there in the midst of our trials, giving us humorous times to refresh us and lift our spirits. When we allow ourselves to be vulnerable with other believers and honestly share our struggles, we are blessed with deeper, more sincere relationships as we lift one another's burdens to our Heavenly Father.

When we consider our relationship with Jesus Christ and the immeasurable gift of salvation He has provided for those who trust in Him, we can learn to be content in any and every situation. If we allow ourselves to be malleable vessels in the hands of the Master Potter, He will use our suffering to reach others. God will bring glory to Himself through our lives if we are willing to be molded and shaped by Him. When we focus on eternity instead of the moment, we are filled with joy as we await the fulfillment of God's promises. We look forward to the redemption of our earthly bodies releasing us from their subjection to death and decay. We have much to look forward to!

1 Thessalonians 5:16-18 instructs us:

> Rejoice always; pray without ceasing; in everything give thanks; for this is God's will for you in Christ Jesus.

When we focus on the benefits of our suffering, we really can give thanks in all things.

I am not the same woman I was when Bradley was born. I am grateful for what the Lord has taught us through Bradley. My commitment to Christ has been strengthened, my relationship with Him deepened, and my knowledge of him increased, although I still have a lot to learn! Through our experiences with Bradley, God has revealed Himself to me in a way I would not have known otherwise. He has proven Himself faithful again and again. He has and will continue to work *in all things* for my good and for the good of my family, because we love and serve Him. With that assurance, we "fight the good fight" (1 Timothy 1:18 & 6:12) and continue on in the task He has assigned for us. With His help and for His glory, we will complete it! Amen!

> Therefore, since we have so great a cloud of witnesses surrounding us, let us also lay aside every encumbrance and the sin which so easily entangles us, and let us run with endurance the race that is set before us, fixing our eyes on Jesus, the author and perfecter of faith, who for the joy set before Him endured the cross, despising the shame, and has sat down at the right hand of the throne of God. For consider Him who has endured such hostility by sinners against Himself, so that you will not grow weary and lose heart (Hebrews 12:1-3).

Heather embracing "Bo" on his 13th birthday

End Notes

[1] "Jesus Wants Me for a Sunbeam," Talbot, Nellie and Excell, Edwin O. 1900, Public Domain.

[2] "Jesus Loves the Little Children," Woolston, C. H. and Root, George. Public Domain.

[3] "Jesus Loves Me," Warner, Anna Bartlett. Philadelphia: J. B. Lippincott & Company, 1860 and Bradbury, William B., 1862. Public Domain.

[4] "Great and Mighty," 1984, Sound III, Inc. (Admin. by MCA Music Publishing).

[5] "He Is Lord," Johnson, Linda Lee; Cloninger, Claire and Fettke, Tom. Nashville: Word, Inc., 1986.

[6] "Victory in Jesus," Bartlett, Eugene M. Powell, Missouri: Albert E. Brumley & Sons, Inc., 1939.

[7] Dr. M. R. DeHaan. *Broken Things*. Grand Rapids: Zondervan, 1948.

Other Titles
from Parson Place Press

For more information regarding discounts, see
www.parsonplacepress.com/store

A Time For Everything (Second Edition)

by Michael White

ISBN 13: 978-0-9842163-6-9

Does God still work miracles today as He did in the Bible?

Seven Keys to Effective Prayer

by Michael L. White

ISBN 13: 978-0-9842163-8-3

Stop hindrances to your prayers now!

The Unseen War: Winning the Fight for Life

by David K. Kortje

ISBN 13: 978-0-9786567-7-5

Spiritual warfare may be one of the most significant aspects of the Christian life.

Seasons of the Heart

by Lori Stratton

ISBN 13: 978-0-9786567-2-0

Let your heart be stirred anew

CPSIA information can be obtained at www.ICGtesting.com
Printed in the USA
BVOW020250220313

316192BV00005B/8/P